Once Upon a Recession

Facing the New Economic Realities with ***Passion, Purpose*** *and* ***Commitment*** *to Succeed!*

BY

Selwa Hamati

WITH

Michelle Gamble-Risley

"Selwa Hamati's book covers important material. She writes lyrically and from the heart."

H. JACKSON PEYTON, PSY.D.,
LICENSED CLINICAL PSYCHOLOGIST

"Selwa has a beautiful compassion for the human spirit. She offers a great road map to support people in connecting to their passion and getting the most out of life despite their circumstances."

BOB FIORETTI, OWNER, INFINITE POSSIBILITIES, LLC

"I am enjoying it. I think it puts together a strategy that we can all use. I like the empowerment of folks to take charge of change. I love the focus on [how to deal with] the recession."

JILL TECHEL, MAYOR, CITY OF NAPA

"This book is an easy to read step by step uplifting story with wonderful examples of how to shift your thinking from negative to positive and focus on opportunities rather than loss. It's the right book for the right time."

DOROTHY SALMON

Library of Congress Control Number: 2010935966

ISBN-13: 9780615403403

Once Upon a Recession soft-cover edition 2010

Printed in the United States of America

For more information about special discounts for bulk purchases, please contact 3L Publishing at 916.300.8012 or log onto our website at www.3LPublishing.com.

Book design by Erin Pace.

This book is dedicated to you, Mom.
Thank you for instilling strong faith and core values
in me. You defied all odds to raise me and my brothers;
and you did a fine job ... I love you!

Acknowledgments

If I mentioned all of you by name, I would need quite a few pages! So I will acknowledge all my mentors — teachers and clients alike. You have provided me the platform on which I present this book; for this I am eternally grateful.

I also want to acknowledge those of you who took time out of your very busy schedules to read through the book, offer suggestions and/or corrections, then write your testimonial so that others can get a glimpse of what it's about. Thank you!

Last, but definitely NOT least, a big THANK YOU to the three most important men in my life ... my wonderful husband, Nicolas, and two awesome sons, Nick and Randy. You know how much I love and appreciate you. Thanks for believing in me!

Contents

Introduction

Someday this recession will end. Sounds almost as pleasant as the lyrics "someday my prince will come" — except we're not waiting for a man (or woman for that matter) to save us. The recession — and maybe it will be over by the time this book hits the market — has been perhaps the greatest opportunity in the last three decades to teach us not only lessons about money and finance, but lessons about self, spirituality and resilience. It has given us an amazing chance to hold the mirror up to our lives and ask some important questions about who we truly are and who we long to be in this world — outside of our traditional definitions of financial success and happiness.

Our generation went from "having it all" to figuring out "how to keep it all" — and then at the end of the day, shedding it *all.* So what the recession has really done is not empty our bank accounts but produce a spiritual awakening for thousands of people who were in some sense ready to transition to something new and more fulfilling; something to feel passionate about; and something that, outside of the physical trappings of the so-called "good life," had long since gone missing. Recession or not, many people may have eschewed those trappings and moved on anyway; but the recession opened the door of providence to push the change faster than some felt comfortable about and, perhaps, regardless of their desire to do so or not.

You may be reading this and thinking, "I loved my old life. I didn't want to lose my job and livelihood for some spiritual awakening." These are common thoughts, but many who lost their jobs and income in the early days of the recession, have already walked a path toward a new life. They understand exactly what we're saying. For them, this book will be an affirmation of their choices and decisions to move forward. For the rest, this book will help you understand that in loss there can be great opportunity followed by gratitude for what appeared to be misfortune. In the 2009 movie *Up in the Air,* Ryan Bingham, the lead character, says, "Anybody who ever built an empire, or changed the world, sat where you are now. And it's because they sat there that they were able to do it."

While it's painful to lose one's job, the silver lining as aptly described by Bingham is the "opportunity" — the opportunity to rise above everything and find a new journey, path or map to a better life. The truth is that 61 percent of Americans hate their jobs — that is, over half of your friends, associates and family *hate* their jobs. If you fall into that 61 percent, do you realize that you're spending your entire adult life doing something you hate? Now if you happen to be one of those 61 percent who also lost a job, do you see the opportunity to change what you hated doing? Maybe you never saw the "out" — the exit strategy to get on a new track and join the 39 percent who do like their jobs or businesses. Are you following your dream? Do you even have a dream to follow? If you don't, when was the last time you stopped to ask yourself: "What do *I* really want?" Now, more than ever, is the time to do just that!

Once Upon a Recession is written to help those struggling to find their way toward their own "economic recovery;" look at their lives differently; figure out how to become resilient if they are not already; and uncover their own "Stimulus Package" for a new future. If you think that life just gave you and dozens of your neighbors some really rancid lemons that couldn't possibly make sweet lemonade, think again. Even when we come out of this recession — and we will — the economy will never be the same. The way people do business … never the same. How you do business … never the same.

Even if you don't want to change, everyone else will have shifted — and many already had begun the transformation even before the economy sank on the scale of the Titanic. Survivors have been affected; however, the recession's influence has, for many, been so emotionally and physically transformational that they have no regret, but rather joy and exhilaration for where the lifeboat landed. You will read stories about the resilient men and women who not just got through it, but did so to come out the other end happier than they could ever have imagined. These are stories about bitter reality, grief, honesty, courage and tenacity to go for it with strength, passion and commitment to succeed.

You will feel inspired — and most importantly motivated and energized to think about your situation in a whole new light. And you will never look at the rancid lemons with the same wrinkled brow ever again. In fact, you will seize the lemons and make the best lemonade ever!

Selwa Hamati
www.DreamPlanAchieve.com

Chapter One

When the Music's Over

"The face in the mirror won't stop
The girl in the window won't drop
A feast of friends
'Alive!' she cried
Waitin' for me
Outside!"
— THE DOORS

"When the music's over … turn out the lights" — lyrics from a great Doors song. Sometimes the lights go out right when you thought you had only gotten midway through your life's song. Many people in the early to mid-2000s were singing, dancing and enjoying economic prosperity. Those in the housing, mortgage and real estate industries in particular had much to revel about. They were working in what appeared to be a prosperous industry where people lined up to purchase houses like they were buying tickets to a rock concert. Anyone who worked in the supporting construction trades, engineering and architectural firms, etc., could party and enjoy unprecedented financial success. Most people didn't foresee the bubble about to burst (at least not as rapidly as it did). Most people didn't predict all party hats off and steamers stomped on. Most people didn't anticipate the dead silence and stunned expressions as the party ended almost as quickly as it started. The money, fun and rush of extreme success was suddenly all gone and evaporated like a dry riverbed. Now all these revelers would face an uncertain freefall that would produce one of the worst recessions in the last 30 years and invite comparisons to the Great Depression.

Some people were so completely caught off guard that it would take them some time to get their bearings around this new, unfamiliar and unpleasant economic reality. If you worked in one of the hardest-hit industries related to the housing market, the writing on the wall came into focus sooner than later. Some life-long real estate experts who knew better and had not gotten involved in the rush to sell low-interest loans and profit from what clearly would fall apart sooner or later had kept their plates clean. They had never gotten caught up in the party, had built loyal customer relationships, and avoided selling loans that they knew on some level might come home to roost in their client base. Yet even those who approached this market with a lot of caution and prudence still got hit pretty hard. This reality that first struck the housing market later acted like a terrible wave to drown out many other industries — and thus, the recession rolled in much like a tsunami in wave after wave after wave.

I was one of those people involved in the real estate industry when the recession hit in its full, unceremonious glory. Like so many people, I was faced with an unfamiliar and unexpected economic reality. It became painfully obvious as the months rolled by and no new work came in that I was about to face something life changing and important. In some ways facing up to your new status as the business owner with no work or the employee with no job seems to go through stages much like grief — denial, anger, depression and, finally, acceptance. When your identity has been completely tied up in a job, career or business and someone comes and says, "Whoops! That's not you anymore," what do you do? Or when you've just quit your job and you set out to conquer the world — to make a big difference — only to discover the world didn't wait for you; the economy shifted before you could get your feet steady on the ground; and now you're emotionally and financially unprepared and don't know how to take your first step forward. You feel your identity being snatched right from beneath your feet. It knocks you completely off balance and sometimes flat on your face. Even the strongest people may feel a horrible sadness and grief take over their lives. What do you do? The answer is often not obvious!

Like most people, at first I waited … living off savings ... and waited. I thought for sure new hope would come and things would change. I waited with pure hopefulness and eager attention to the news and stock market. A new sun would surely rise. It had to, right? My savings were gone and work wasn't coming in; now what? Vigilance and fortitude alone will buy you absolutely nothing when you, like everyone else, only hold on. You can barricade yourself into the notion that the outside world that seemingly controls your destiny will change, and therefore, so will your checking account. You can do what most everyone else does: get in the unemployment line, complain there are no jobs, and accept your unemployment check as the last solution to your unsolvable problem.

A solution, mind you, that may barely help you make your bill payments — and hopefully you have some kind of support system to subsidize your balance. Otherwise, run up the credit cards and loans and melt the gold jewelry.

This traditional road to acceptance seemed initially like the answer to my problem. It certainly appeared to be an acceptable answer to many other people's economic woes. The degree of acceptance varied, of course. Those who worked for the state of California, for example, and were furloughed seemed to assume the stance of acceptance pretty well. After all, they still had jobs while many others were unpleasantly unemployed. Between the never-ending bad news of ever-increasing layoffs and state workers finding a new, unexpected "day off," everything around me seemed to scream — *get used to it!*

Now out of denial, I would have to get used to a new way of life. I would have to face the loss of this career identity. I would have to face the scorn and "I told you so's" of my well-meaning circle of family and friends. Perhaps I would have to get in the unemployment line and wait my turn — that is what "everyone" had to do. We have to get *used* to it. Adjusting to this new way of life seemed inextricably inevitable. Acceptance meant reshaping my life, adjusting my spending, changing my habits — long-sown habits that felt really great too. I mean an incredible afternoon at the spa always sounds way better than a long-drawn-out afternoon waiting in the unemployment line. Yet this "new normal" just kind of set in like life always seems to do.

It's not terribly surprising what you can get used to — waking up to start the "new normal" all over again. Calling and networking with a singular hope that maybe the real estate well wasn't so obviously dry. Maybe I could keep on keeping on. You know how it goes. You tell yourself, you'll just face the economic storm head-on. And some part of that thinking (as you'll see) will be helpful, but what is not helpful is acceptance of the negative and so-called "new normal" that can take over your life — your train of thought. If you pay attention, you will find that the media-controlled thought process can eventually erode the last piece of hope and dignity you retain deep inside. The media-declared bad economy changes mindsets, corrodes hopefulness, and can challenge even the most positive person.

Let me ask you this question: Why, if the music ended on that CD called your career and life, did you automatically assume you would just find a way to restart the same old tune? Maybe now in the middle of all this I, like many others around me, needed a huge wake-up call. Maybe it's really time to analyze the identity you had given yourself via a career or business. How is it working for you now? And back to the introduction, did you even like that career? Sixty-one percent of you right now are shaking your heads. Yet here I stood — and here you may stand — weeping over the loss of it. Let's set the record straight: You're crying about something you hated? Is that right? Why would you automatically pursue rebuilding something you hated? Or let's say you did love it, and you're crying for the belief that it's lost forever. Is it *really?*

Once Upon a Recession is my love story for all the unemployed, furloughed and disenfranchised workers and business owners out there who are ready for change. When the "music is over" don't turn out the lights and start wailing as if you've lost your beloved. This recession — this time in history — has given you an unbelievable opportunity to rethink your life. Do you understand this concept? Now more than ever our culture is in the middle of a tremendous spiritual and metaphysical shift into something greater — something beyond the shallow trappings of perceived wealth, money and financial success. Many of us had it all. Many of us, consciously or not — like me — lost our souls to the material world and fell into self-constructed traps based on perceptions of what or who we should be in this world. The recession has created an opening in the universal spirit of humanity for reaching forbidden dreams or being wholly reinvented and transformed in incredible and unexpected ways. If you can just get past old notions about who you thought you were tied to this job or business that is not what it used to be anymore.

It sounds so hard, doesn't it? It is especially difficult for those men and women who are not just facing up to job or business loss, but have managed to skate through. If you were *fortunate* — yes, I said fortunate — enough to be drowned in the first wave, you are blessed! Did you hear me? *Blessed!* You are so far ahead of everyone else in this new transformation, and you will be that much more enlightened and aware when the economy does come around … and it *will* — mark these words, it always does. This economic transformation has changed and impacted lives in so many different ways!

Even now at what could be the tail end of the recession, attitudes and beliefs are shifting. What we will be "when we grow" into our next self and our new life is not going to be the same. If you can just open your mind to what we're going to share about resilience, rebirth and re-imagining your dreams you will see the lessons learned in the last three years as heartening and important to your new YOU. You will feel exactly the way I do. I am gleefully and happily changed — heart and soul. I've redefined, reinvented my life, and pursued a new course. And I have the God-blessed recession to thank for it!

Can you imagine? I am grateful for the recession of all things. Why? Because had I not been knocked down and kicked around by an economic storm on scale with a hurricane, I would have stayed right where I was. I would have no incentive to reflect; ask myself some very important, life-changing questions; and reinvent a whole new life strategy that paves a new road to something beyond special — my happiness and good fortune. Good fortune that has some to do with financial bliss, but more importantly to do with spiritual calm, peace and tranquil joy. It can be yours too. Just keep reading.

Chapter Two

What Doesn't Kill Us Makes Us Recession Proof

"Twenty years from now you will be more
disappointed by the things that you didn't do
than by the ones you did do.
So throw off the bowlines.
Sail away from the safe harbor.
Catch the trade winds in your sails.
Explore. Dream. Discover."
— MARK TWAIN

Wasn't it our mothers who told us, "That which doesn't kill us makes us strong?" Most people would probably admit that they would rather just be "weak" than be unceremoniously forced to face up to some harsh realities. Who needs to be *that* strong, right? In fact, it seems much more pleasant to just enjoy great fortune and success than to be dumped into a nasty reality brought on by circumstances that, to some, seem outside of their control. There, in that statement, lies the deep fallacy that often *controls* us!

These same "nasty" circumstances can force us to the proverbial mental gym to strengthen our emotional and intellectual muscles, and hence make us stronger. In the reality of today's economy, many of us have been forced to face the harsh reality that business may not come as easily as it did four years ago; jobs may be lost that were once rewarding and vibrant career opportunities; work must now be done for less money; and some cash-strapped individuals may take up to two or three jobs to be able to just survive. These realities — the truth of today's economy — have also forced some people to ask important questions and take a moment to reflect on the next step. And maybe not just continue as-is and be content with the status quo, but rather re-evaluate their lives. Who do you want to be now? Was that really you before? Or is this a rare chance to seize the opportunity and change your life? How will you show up in the world now that you have no other choice but to change something?

You see, the true "economic fallout" for many has turned into a blessing disguised as hardship. At first, it seems like a terrible blow to lose one's job. You feel like you've really lost your way; but the light hidden in the trauma — or perceived trauma — is an opportunity for a deeper awakening. Your strength builds from asking yourself some fundamental questions before you cry and begrudgingly pull out your 10-year-old resume to overhaul it. The time is now. You are at a true juncture in the split road — and to continue as-is without reflection and choice is not the decision of strength but desperation.

Fear of the unknown, and fear of it getting worse than it already appears can be a terrible driver, for example, to just stick to the course that seems obvious. If you were a truck driver just try and find a new truck-driving company and apply. Or if, like me, you were a real estate agent, just keep trying to sell houses as the market falls apart. Many people decided to turn a blind eye to the lack of business and try to climb the mountain, as it seemingly grows taller and taller with no peak in sight. The first thing to understand in all of this is how to pull yourself up by the bootstraps and be resilient. Resilience is what will guide and save you from falling into a deeper hole of troubles. Within resilience you will find your way. And resilience is truly the first step toward the light.

I didn't "figure it out" — all of what I'm about to share — overnight. I've read some really great books among them *Think and Grow Rich* by Napoleon Hill, *The Success Principles* by Jack Canfield, *The Four Agreements* by Don Miguel Ruiz, *The Secret* by Rhonda Byrne, *The Power of Now* by Eckhart Tolle, *The Science of Getting Rich* by Wallace Wattles, and many more; I've attended seminars, enrolled in courses, and obtained certifications that help me along my path to live my purpose. I learned a lot about my own power — or shall I say "self empowerment" — to not just get through the storms, but also come out the other side better than before and truly become enlightened. What's really fantastic about the information I'm going to share is that while it whole-heartedly applies to the recession, it really applies to life in general. So what you are about to learn to help change your life and turn around your reality will become your own wonderful life journey.

We can all "get through" the hard times, but we may not be wiser or better off for it. We may have just climbed the mountain only to get to the top and gaze across at all the other "mountains" in the range — an endless journey. We certainly don't feel inspired, motivated or even prepared to move onto a blissful destination; but I want to caution you from the start … I'm not saying that once I give you the tools your journey will suddenly become clear and easy; that you'll never face any challenges (like the recession) — you will inevitably face them, because that is life.

What I am doing is giving you tools and new ways of looking at things so that one day, when you find yourself sitting in a chaise lounge on some tropical beach and peacefully looking back on your life, you'll feel good about yourself — your choices, decisions, experiences … all of it! You will know that you did your best, walked in your integrity, and strived for excellence; you made things happen, so you wouldn't have to wonder what happened! No regrets. No demons. Simple acknowledgement and acceptance — all your foibles and humanity, all your greatness, and all your wonderfulness rolled up into a singular life experience. A life you can feel proud to have lived. And oddly enough, you can thank the recession of today for helping you move to a higher level of thinking and being … *tomorrow.*

So what are the basic principles to recession proof your life — principles that help you become super resilient and able to take on the world? In a basic and fundamental sense, resilience requires:

- Acknowledgement of authentic truth
- Ownership or responsibility
- Commitment to change
- Reprogramming your thoughts
- Courage to actually change
- Staying the course (persistence)
- Reaping the rewards!

ACKNOWLEDGEMENT OF AUTHENTIC TRUTH

Why did I use the phrase "authentic truth" versus just truth? Our society imposes all kinds of cultural rules and restrictions that often keep us from being our "authentic" selves. Authenticity — a well-covered topic in a book titled *Be Yourself: Everybody Else is Taken* by Mike Robbins — explores the importance of being your authentic self. Robbins says, "Authenticity is the buzzword of the moment. 'Be true to yourself.' 'Be your real self.' The message is loud and clear. Or is it? There is pressure from all around (our parents, teachers, spouses, co-workers, friends and the media) telling us it's more important to be liked and to fit in than it is to be who we truly are. We are also constantly bombarded with messages that we aren't good enough and need to be "fixed." Robbins' book is funny, self-effacing, but above all — honest.

So when I considered the subject of "telling your

truth," I realized our so-called truth can be mired in so many societal pressures, demands for conformity, and peer pressure to be "normal." First, as you're going through this process with me, I don't care one bit about any of those things. I am much more concerned that you be honest — not with me or your family and friends — but with yourself. So, when I say the first principle of resilience involves truth — I mean the real truth — even the nasty, blistering and smelly *authentic* part of the truth; the kind you may not want to write home about, but that you need to bring out in the open. No judgment will come from me nor should you sit as your own judge and jury. Just "get real" within!

Authenticity means genuine — the real thing. So your authentic truth must come from the real you — the person who inside *knows* what's what. Again, no need for a confessional or tribunal to force your story out in the open, just start by quietly asking, "How do I really want to ***be*** in the world?" You may find the journey toward resilience diverted in other directions too — distracted by self-deception; but you cannot start to bounce back and find a new path without first acknowledging you've lost your way. Authentic truth requires us to see it, acknowledge it, and change how we deal with it.

OWNERSHIP OR RESPONSIBILITY

I know we've all heard the phrase, "Take responsibility for your life." OK, you've heard it a zillion times, but have you done it? You can't change anything or do anything about an important issue in your life if you're not willing to own it. Oh no — that's not my problem, right? OK, so your life has gone to hell and you've lost your job — and again hell hath levels that have nothing to do with fire or brimstone. Hell can be as simple as being stuck in a miserable rut where you can't remember the last time you laughed so hard your gut hurt. Hell is a bad marriage where you fight more than you agree and have no physical connection anymore. Hell is a bad boss that treats you like an idiot and hasn't given you a raise in two years (and uses the economy as an excuse while he continues to fly in his corporate jet). Hell is also pure boredom.

So, hell hath no fury like a life gone wrong. And whose life is it anyway? Pretty darned sure it's not your friend's life. So, let's digress for a moment. If you don't take responsibility, then you've abdicated your power and ... yuck! You've assumed the powerless "victim" role. I think it's sad when people fall into a subservient role of victimization. You know victims have lost their power, right? They gave the keys to their kingdom to some invisible king or queen they've never met, but clearly and willingly (though often unconsciously/robotically) gave "it up" in exchange for a powerless title.

You are no victim! Please do yourself and everyone else a favor — own your life. Victimization shifts responsibility to external, uncontrollable forces (e.g. it's the recession's fault!). It says, "I don't have any power in my life. Everyone does it *to and against me.* And I had nothing to do with it." How many ways can I pull that line of thinking apart to demonstrate why it won't work for successful, satisfied living? Understand that victims blame everyone for what happens to them. They live in the proverbial world of "I'm right" and "you're wrong." Actually "the WHOLE world is wrong!" It's always someone else's fault not theirs. Wow! Look at what I just wrote. If these people (victims) are so righteous, why then are they so miserable? Why have their lives gone off the tracks? A righteous person should clearly be on the "right" path. Yet here they are — unhappy, possibly spiritually broken, and blaming the world for how they arrived on discontented rock. If I hadn't gotten laid off; if I hadn't been furloughed; if I didn't have to work two jobs; if I could just catch a break — and the list goes on.

Let me tell you something, my dear reader, "quit blaming your troubles on everyone else. You do play an active role. You make choices. You make decisions. No one makes right choices all the time; so if you find yourself in a "bad" situation, stop and evaluate it, and then you can make an educated decision based on facts at hand. Learn from your mistakes and move on. If you're on a trip and you take the wrong exit, do you keep on going anyway — all the while cussing out the freeway signs, the truck that blocked your view, the directions your friend gave you, etc., etc.? I sure hope not! You turn around or stop and ask for directions; bottom line, you correct the situation and move on. Why? Because you want to get to your destination.

So the lowdown: If you made choices — decisions to do something with your life that for one reason or another didn't work out — shifting responsibility and blame to someone else doesn't erase one clear fact: You **participated**. OK, enough said.

Taking responsibility plays a powerful role on your journey toward resilience — and you will be amazed to discover that it feels really good to do it. In fact, I am willing to say, it's easier to own it than to abandon it somewhere — it WILL come back to haunt you! *If you can't own it, you can't fix it; and if you can't fix it, you can't make it work.*

COMMITMENT TO CHANGE

Commitment to change sounds easy on the surface. I am committed to change ______________________________ (fill in the blank). You can sit around and cry "commitment" to your friends and family but actions speak louder than words. Do you know that the ability to honor your commitment might be the hardest part of resilience? Why, you ask? Because honoring the commitment to anything is where the good stuff starts — it's the place where the lip service turns into something special. I could sit in a room full of dozens of "committed" folks who want to change their lives, but they somehow spin in circles while professing their whole-hearted and genuine desire to be different and/or to do things differently. They might show up time and time again at our workshops, eager to go through the planning process, yet still walk away with a piece of paper, and no real commitment to put any of it into action. (We do workshops for my contributing writer Michelle Gamble-Risley's book *Second Bloom: 10 Steps to Reinvent, Rejuvenate and Realize a New Life* and for my own workshop, called *'Mind' Your Wellness.*)

When you make a down-and-dirty commitment to resilience, persistence and perseverance become your friends. You honor your commitment to your ideals. You don't let other people dissuade you from your goals. You don't waver, waffle or cower back to your awful "comfort" zone. You simply focus and persist.

Michelle, who has her own story to weave into this

book, left corporate America after roughly 15 years of successfully running other people's companies only to trade off her life and family (sound familiar?). She, like I, has learned the value of commitment and staying the course (figure out what that may be for you). Her commitment to start her own business became a passion-driven, all-consuming journey where she vowed to never consider a trip back to "corporate hell" or working for a thankless boss (her last one she now dubs "Captain Crazy"). She declares during any hard times, "I'll eat Top Raman before I'll ever work for another company." Her commitment is clear — she understands she must stay the course and not be diverted or distracted by "escape" routes or "fallbacks" such as taking another job. She's now been independent for four years — and well over the first-year "hump" when most businesses fail.

What makes Michelle or me different? We understand that we must commit ourselves to living the life we love; we must keep our eyes on the game; and we must not be distracted by things like fear or anxiety (we'll discuss those issues later in the book). We must go the distance to enjoy the payoff (remembering to take in and learn from every experience along the way). If you can't honor that kind of commitment, then your likelihood of failure increases one-hundred-fold.

REPROGRAMMING YOUR THOUGHTS

I love the Laws of Attraction. You can read about them in the iconic books *The Science of Getting Rich* and *The Secret*. The basic premise — we attract both positive and negative things into our lives through our thoughts. If you don't want bad things to happen, don't focus on bad things. If you were to walk into a dark room, thinking about the darkness does not get rid of it — you can stand there all day thinking that it's dark and wishing that this darkness would go away; you can complain about it; stumble around in it; and even form a "coalition against darkness" — will any of these things get rid of the darkness? NO, absolutely not! You must think LIGHT and seek the light. It only takes a little bit of light and the darkness begins to disappear.

If you want to attract positive things into your life — health, happiness, money, etc. — then you must think positive about these things. Listen to what you say — because your words mirror the rhetoric in your head and what you're attracting. Here is a case study about a woman who owns a skin-care salon. During the course of a single conversation, she confessed, "She couldn't afford it" about 15 times (no kidding). At the end of the session, her client grabbed her hand, looked her straight in the eye, and said, "If you declare to the Universe you can't afford it. Guess what? The Universe will do everything possible to make that real — and you're right, 'You can't afford it.'"

Now, people act skeptical and don't always agree with the tenets of *The Secret*, but I have personally seen the power of the Laws of Attraction in motion. I used to have this fixed thought that I made money once a month in client payments. One day I thought, "Why do I think checks only come once a month? Why not have money given to me every day?" The moment I shifted how I thought money should come to me, guess what? Money started arriving in my e-mail and my mailbox every day. I seriously started having clients shove money at me. Imagine! I haven't done any work yet but they want to cut me a check on the spot. Wow! All I did was shift how I believed money should come to me. I "reprogrammed" my thoughts. I *changed* a staple way of believing.

Resilience requires a shift in your thinking. If you have not practiced disciplines like the Laws of Attraction, which include assuming gratitude for all things, then you may be stuck in a lot of negativity that affects your life. Later in the book, I am going to give you some specific tools to help you reprogram your thoughts. Assuming control over your thoughts and believing in your ability to attract great things into your life are powerful resources you can use as you resiliently make changes. Reprogramming your inner thought process has potent and often very tangible results (e.g., all that money). So you must understand resilience involves a lot of positive, uplifting thinking — and most importantly — the ability to break the strong hold of negative thinking on your life. The skin-care gal never blinked as her broken record played out of her mouth over and over again. It took an outsider to point it out to her (what a blessing — we need more people who are graciously honest with us).

Friends, beware of the deeply ingrained negative verbiage you have recorded in your head. It's time to erase it and record over it ... you must replace it! (I'll teach you how in later chapters.)

COURAGE TO ACTUALLY CHANGE

I think this principle may be one of the hardest on the list. Many people live their lives in a perpetual state of fear. They use their fear to make up stories as to why they can or cannot do something. Spiritual leader Wayne Dyer has a marvelous presentation he gave on PBS about *Excuses Begone!* (a great book for your library). He discusses how we use this list of deeply engrained beliefs (most of them are fear-based) to avoid making changes in our lives. I'm not going to get into all of the excuses he lists, but one of them was the old excuse, "I can't afford it." Dyer says, "You can afford anything you want." He is absolutely right. The real mystery behind the fears and the excuses is how really irrational all of them become when you delve deeply into the root cause (fear). When you make an excuse or conjure up a reason why you can't prevail — why you're not strong enough, smart enough, or rich enough to move forward — ask yourself, "What am I so afraid of?" What is really stopping me from pursuing the life I wish I were living? Again, we're going to fully explore the power of fear later in the book.

In the meantime, you need to consciously pull out what holds you back from changing and improving your life? Resilient people know how to bend fluidly and change to find their way. They don't get caught up in fear-based constructs that continually hold them back. They have more courage than David had when he faced Goliath. They are not mightier or stronger, but perhaps wiser and more willing to see what's around the corner with an open curiosity versus a nervous peek followed by eyes closed and a jump backward. It takes resilience and a lot of courage to change. It takes real confidence and certainty that you can do anything (you have everything within you right now to achieve all of your goals and dreams ... and then some). You can attract whatever you need when you *decide* to move in the direction of your dreams. Resilience means that when you encounter fear — and we all do — you don't cower away and run for "safety." You're only running back to your familiar circumstances — often not so safe! You must face fear head on, eyes forward, and with a swift stride right into the eye of the force. You know deep within yourself you can do anything when you have a burning desire to do it.

Fearlessness of that caliber makes miracles out of lives. It turns former treasurers or real estate agents into authors and coaches (my "dream" life). It takes ideas conjured in the imagination of the fearless and turns them into solid gold success. And when you have attained whatever miracle or magic you seek, you will look back and realize all of the fear was just a smoke screen that, if allowed to, would waste your life away. None of your darkest "monsters" came out of the closet. Your house didn't fall down. The sky didn't plummet on your head. You didn't *lose* your life savings or destroy your family. Every deep dark worry you've stored up and used as the almighty whip to keep you securely locked up in a cage of your own design never came to fruition. I swear on whatever resembles your good book when you courageously make change and go for your dreams, everything will be fine. I promise! Who made up the rule that change is scary? *Really?*

Why? Why can't change be magnificent? As a matter of fact, it is! So have the courage to change and see what happens.

Note: Please don't take the above encouragement as an excuse (yet again) to make abrupt decisions that are not good for you or the people you care about. You may still need to keep a part-time "job" until your business gets going; but you really must be disciplined, focused, and committed to your #1 goal: plan, prioritize and take action that will advance you in the direction of your goal(s) every single day.

STAYING THE COURSE

Now, you may feel inspired, motivated and ready to move forward with your life. You may have dreams of real Sugar Plum fairies sprinkling good fortune on you. You may have pulled yourself up by the bootstraps and hoisted your behind out of the muck. You stand tall and prepared. You're going to quit that nasty job; you're going to get out of a bad relationship; you're going to face life with a clear mind; you're going to meet someone new; you're going to start a new business ... whatever your heart's desire, you're energized and ready to meet the challenge. And then ... oh no, the first barrier sneakily barges into the middle of your road and sits its big rock behind in your way. Now I want to whisper in your ear how having the *"ability to stay the course"* will help you foist the rock out of your way rather than make a decision to sit down on the rock and eat your lunch.

A man named Jon was determined to start his own business as a general contractor. He absolutely didn't want to work for his foreman anymore. He wanted to be a business owner. He took the first step and quit his job. Within months, he had a little work; but over time, Jon got distracted. His wife needed help with her client retention business, so Jon started helping her out three days a week. Three days soon turned to four, and before Jon knew it he wasn't minding his own store anymore. By the time he put his attention back on his business, his few clients had gotten too frustrated and left. Rather than face the inevitable challenge of starting over, Jon allowed himself to be distracted by a fallback — taking a job with another company. He figured he would build up his resources and get started again. Jon took that job two years ago. He still works for someone else — course permanently diverted — and momentum wasted and probably never to be built up again. Jon didn't understand the importance of *staying the course.* He took a permanent lunch break on the rock in the road. He sort of made a half-hearted attempt to move it, but not really. The minute he thought, "Wow ... too hard," he moved onto something else. He didn't realize his dream. He still comes home every night and complains about his new boss.

You can't become resilient until you realize that rocks need to be moved — and not all rocks break your back; actually most don't. You will likely find that as you move through the experience of understanding that "rocks" are only meant as tests — a way of testing your resilience, your commitment, your faith, and your ability to stay the course — you will be amazed to realize that those rocks shrink to pebbles over time until one day you literally flick them away. I know, I know — it sounds way too simple. Truly, friends, I mean every word. Just try living your life the way I've recommended, and it all starts to function like this fine-tuned machine meant to literally shove you toward success. I always tell people, "Trust the magic. Don't try to analyze it." Find a way around, over, under or through your obstacles.

REAPING THE REWARDS

Now we come to my favorite principle — reaping the rewards. Resilience — once understood and attained — has unimaginable outcomes. When you prevail over your obstacles and move in the right direction, you will enjoy a life you never thought possible. I wake up every day and thank God I got it together (finally! And always striving to be better). Thank God for the big stuff, and thank God for the small stuff. Thank Him for helping me discover the amazing woman He so lovingly created! Won't you begin your own process of discovery? You will be awed and humbled by the amazing creation YOU are!

Chapter Three

What Are You Going to do About it? Create a Vision and an Action Plan

"I think there is something more important than believing: action! The world is full of dreamers, there aren't enough who will move ahead and begin to take concrete steps to actualize their vision."
— W. CLEMENT STONE

What is a resilient life without a vision? You can certainly learn to be resilient and keep going, but I ask you, "Toward what? To what end?" Why do you bother at all if you don't have a sense of purpose and a powerful vision to guide you? Did you really read that question? It's the "why-bother" part that should jump at you. Without a true, clear and necessary (and I mean necessary) vision, you will stumble into the why-bother category of living. When you lose a job or you're furloughed or you're just tired of the trap of a go-nowhere career, you can end up feeling like your life landed on the "why-bother" scrap pile. I mean *really,* why bother? When you feel a lack of vision, purpose or passion, you can easily succumb to inner fears, give into anger, and forget to see the beauty all around you. You can lose a grasp of the happiness factor and misplace joy.

"Why bother" has a limp, lackluster sound to it. Who cares? Why bother? If I don't care then I won't be disappointed, and I won't have to commit to anything meaningful — including my own wellbeing. I simply fall into the ugly get-by track where I follow the bland road to "Nothing-Ville." I bet many of you are nodding, but also thinking, "Why should I bother?" Hence, the need for a vision, a goal, a new picture of where you want to go, and who you want to be — something to motivate, inspire and guide you.

Most people struggling to find their way try to drum up a sense of resilience to keep moving, but they continue to struggle. Since struggling is NO fun, they find it almost impossible to hold on to their dreams. Why is it so hard to hold on? Because they lack a clear vision and, most importantly, the belief that they can and indeed deserve to live that vision.

A vision acts as a compass. When you think about it, the most resilient of people have a clear vision of what they keep picking up their behinds over and over again to do. They feel a sense of empowerment, and resilience becomes their hand on the throttle to thrust toward something important and meaningful (to them). Without a strong sense of purpose and passion, you may flounder and fall. Your energy wanes; your ambition diminishes; and your desire fails. A powerful vision turns it around. Your energy rises; your ambition increases; and your desire ascends. You feel not just ready but fully prepared to overcome any obstacles that may block your way.

A vision serves as your personal catalyst, motivator and inspirational tool to move forward. Some people borrow money, lose money, win and lose jobs — but all the while have absolutely no vision or purpose in life. When you are fortunate enough to have a vision, it will help you find your way and act as an important compass. I took some coaching classes while I was still doing real estate and felt inspired — and that inspiration led me to start my business: "Selwa Hamati and Associates," and later to write this book. I wanted to help other people find their way and use that all-important compass to guide them. I seized the idea that I would write this book and wrapped my head around a bigger goal — to use the book as a platform for speaking engagements and workshops.

I created my vision, and then I took one very important step. I created my vision board. I pasted my dreams on my board and used that vision board to keep squarely in my head what I'm striving to achieve. By the way, I'm definitely not staking the claim that I am the mastermind behind the vision or the board for that matter. Books like *The Secret* cover that subject much more thoroughly, but I want to emphasize the power of vision and the need for the support of the vision board (or notebook — whatever works for you; I suggest a combination of the two) to remind you of your goals — especially when you're having some hard days.

So how do you define or find your vision? So many people just don't know how. Even when I explain what I'm about to dig into here, they still struggle. When I speak to groups, I like to suggest they honestly answer the age-old question, "If I had a $1 million (well, more like $10 million with today's costs), what would I do with the rest of my life?" Remember that question? Guidance counselors loved to ask it. Well, what would you do? Or better yet, would you do what you're doing now? Let's say probably not.

If I had $10 million I can tell you right now I would still be doing what I'm doing. So, my $10-million answer reinforces that I'm on track. Your $10-million answer may be very revealing to help you define your vision. I can suggest what your answer won't include: time spent doing a job that kills your enthusiasm and passion; time wasted on a bad marriage or relationship; or any other issue that makes you miserable. Or the really big one — the trap millions of people fall into — the get-by-to-get-by lifestyle consisting of boredom, lack of interest, loss of energy, and generally nothing to jump out of bed about. Remember, you don't have to experience anything extreme to find your life has just drifted into a meaningless haze. As a matter of fact, just coasting along is the most dangerous enemy of all; it's just not uncomfortable enough. Extreme experiences can shake some sense into us, if we let them — if we're open to receiving the lesson.

You probably heard about the experiment with frogs. If a frog is put in a pot of cold water and the water is heated slowly, the frog will stay in there until it boils to death (it adjusts to the temperature as it heats up a *little* bit at a time and stays "comfy cozy" in there). However, if a frog is thrown in a pot of boiling water, it jumps right out! Are you going to gradually get used to the status quo until it eventually kills your soul? Or are you going to feel the heat (danger) and get out before it's too late?

BE BOLD! BE FEARLESS!

So finding a vision or an idea that would empower you to get on with it plays an incredible and powerful role in your resilience process. Your vision shouldn't be some meager idea you drum up out of desperation to find one. Your vision must be based on something that you really, *really* want. If you want something badly enough — really, REALLY want it — you will keep moving forward and upward toward what you want no matter what obstacles get in your way, even if you stumble and fall hundreds of times. Form your vision without fear, anxiety, trepidation or questions like, "Can I afford it?" "What if I fail?" "What if I can't do it?" No, friends! Your vision should be a full-on embrace of remembered or almost forgotten dreams — where something deep inside is crying out, wishing to be heard. This "something" is the truth — your truth — your real inner desires waiting to be fulfilled. You must not wax or wane on any unanswered questions or fears, but completely surrender your soul to pure, unequivocal truth. What would you like to be doing more than anything in the world? Come on! Everyone has an answer to this question, but 90 percent of us are afraid to even think about it; so we make excuses or dismiss the possibility as not being real. I'm asking you right now to have a "get-real" moment. Set all of the nonsense aside and find out what you really, really want to do with the rest of your life, starting from right here, right now.

Now, allow me to give you a clear warning. Whatever the vision, you can attain it. But, you need to know that the journey toward realizing your vision has two important truths you must willingly understand and embrace. First, you have to be flexible, open minded and, most importantly, resilient at all times — "go with the flow" of your journey (not following the crowd kind of "going with the flow"). Be forewarned: The journey never takes the same route even if you try to do things the same way every time. Life doesn't work that way! Do you understand? Life, the Universe and God are energy, and you never know how energy will shift, what doors will open; what doors will close; and where you might end up. It doesn't mean you don't keep your eye squarely on your goals, and your heart tuned in to your vision, but just allow life to take you somewhere wonderful (everything is wonderful when you see it through a positive lens) and flow somewhere else ... all the while moving you toward your vision.

Second, your destination may or may not look exactly like the picture you had in mind. You see, the picture hardly ever turns out how we drew it in our heads; but it doesn't mean it won't turn out — and perhaps even better than we imagined. This is where the magic happens ... in the common everyday shifts and changes that come in unexpected ways. When you feel the pain of disappointment and you lose faith in your vision (we all struggle from time to time; it's human nature), remind yourself of the process — understand it, and stay the course just a little longer, because this is when ... wham! God shoves the answer right in your face, and here you find yourself smack in the middle of what you envisioned! At times, we all get so focused on exactly what we want and how we want it to happen that we miss the most obvious, BIG, wide-open door on our path ... this is when God has to step in and get our attention! When the magic weaves throughout your daily life, you know it. You will stand in wonder; but let me share ... don't try and figure it out. God has the overall blueprint. Don't try and read it. Just keep going. From where you are, you can't see the whole picture (you're in it). So let the "Master Designer" work out the plan — he has the sky view.

So you see the significance and the need for your vision. You see that whatever vision you devise you must make it mean something powerful to you. You must make that vision so important you become like a dog with a really great chew toy that refuses to give it up. You will use this vision to lock down your reason to be resilient when the tough times come — and, friends, they will come! You must be absolutely committed and prepared to defend your vision. And most importantly (and this is HUGE) walk stridently through your visionary door when it opens — and believe me those who live with passion and purpose and commitment to their dreams will have the door open at just the right moment; however, many of you will stare dumbfounded at that big, beautiful and bodacious door and manage to slam it shut all on your own. You may or may not realize you just did either.

WHEN THE DOOR OPENS, TAKE ACTION — WALK THROUGH

I want to speak to you now about why you may not walk through it. You may be so stuck in fear; you're paralyzed. The door may open with its bright, golden rays of sunlight to drench your soul, and you may just stand there as your own self-doubt, worry and pain hold you back. You want desperately to walk through that door, but you cannot (at least you *think* you cannot).

Let me tell you a story about a woman we'll call Brenda, who had to torture herself one more time before she learned her lesson. After finally leaving an awful 10-year corporate job, she jumped right back on the train to take yet another job with another loon of a boss before finally overcoming her fear of starting a business. The last crazy situation got so insane, so out-of-control, the door practically swung open in her face. She literally had no other choice but to finally walk through it. And what waited on the other side? Success! Unbelievable, easy-to-attain success that many only dream about, yet she achieved it. Every single fear, tear and hand-wringing moment played out in her head never ever came to pass! This is when I like to remind you, my reader, that you must notice how quickly you (me … all of us) build the nightmare. I want you to practice building your dream, NOT some off-the-wall nightmare based on false ideas, habits and paradigms!

Don't be like Brenda. When the door opens, don't close it. See and recognize that the door has swung open. The opportunity has come for you to live your vision. You absolutely MUST walk through the door. In taking action and moving forward, you are being an active participant in your journey. You are not sitting back and waiting for something or someone to give you answers or make it real for you. You are the sprinter on your own track, the driver of your car, the operator of the machinery that is your life.

THE BEAUTIFUL WORD "HOW"

Now you must understand the "how to:" how to achieve your vision, how to take action, and what action to take. It means learning how to change old patterns of thinking so you can establish new ways of being positive; which means going back to your answers to the "why not?" Why not travel to Europe? Old answer: I can't afford it. Flip the negative over — I CAN afford it — then proceed to plan ahead. Wayne Dyer said it best, "We can afford anything we want," which is mentioned earlier in the book.

So put the negative of affordability through positive, rose-colored glasses that suggest abundance and possibility rule the universe. "God wants us all to live in abundance," says Wallace Wattles in the *Science of Getting Rich* (incidentally Wattles doesn't equate "riches" with wealth in the financial sense — although it involves financial wealth too). God doesn't want us to deprive ourselves. God doesn't want to punish, judge or cast us into harsh poverty and keep beauty and love from us. We might think that deprivation and withhold or lack offer universal truths when, in fact, abundance, overflow and wealth provide the real backdrop to our lives. Nothing in the world really suggests otherwise. Consider that everything we could ever need exists and will always exist for us. *We just have to take action to first understand, grab hold and believe*. Believe God means abundance to be ours. Believe we deserve abundance. Believe we shall have abundance. And then with love and gratitude, say "thank you."

We can take old ideas about deprivation, cannot, will not, and turn them into how to, will do, and move through. You can afford everything. You can do anything. You can be all things. Toss out the no, not and will not and reverse them through the power of positivity. It is happening. I can do it. I am OK. I am successful. I am learning how to … I will not allow fear of the unknown; fear of what has not come to pass and may never come to pass; or fear of negative or unattractive outcomes to filter into my world. I console myself with how I get up and get on with it and comfort myself with the pure reality of the moment where I'm perfectly OK and nothing bad has come to pass or will ever come to pass; but that I learn to navigate my life's journey in an active, positive and productive manner; and I understand that I am not at the mercy of invisible and intangible threats. I will not become consumed by what doesn't exist, because only when I imagine negativity does it show up; but when I imagine I will be OK and I will move forward, I always do. And when I take the reins of my mind and I steer my thoughts toward understanding the world's offerings, I can take those gifts and enjoy life.

THE POWER OF A PLAN

Next up, make a plan — consider the "why not" and turn it into "how to" (which way and when). You have to *be a part of the solution not the problem.* Stop focusing on the problem. I lost my job. I hate my boss. I have an unhappy marriage. I can't take a vacation. Friends, where will this thinking get you? So you're stating facts, now what are you going to do about them? Either through cultural or family training, we have somehow latched onto ruminating and bathing in the issue versus figuring out a plan to change it. Have you ever noticed people who just wallow in the problem mud? They get caught up in what diminishes their desire to move forward and keeps them swirling around in the mess.

When you wallow in a problem, it bogs your mind down. You get sort of hard wired as your mind loops around on the issue at hand. Ever notice if you have trouble sleeping what your mind starts getting stuck on? Silence in the middle of the night gives the mind ample opportunity to playback your worries and fears like some stuck record — over and over again. When you change your view, plan and problem solve, the repetitiveness of the same-old line stops. You focus instead on the "how to" solve the problem; how to move through the problem toward the solution. How do I find a new job?

What kind of a job do I want? How do I improve or end a bad relationship? How do I make my life better?

A guy got laid off — a situation many Americans experience in these times — we'll call him John. John feels really down about no longer having a job. He sits in his house and watches endless Daytime television. His friend asks him, "Hey, John, how is it going?" He says it's terrible out there. He watches depressing news shows that drone about the banks falling apart; GM going bankrupt; and the housing market taking a plunge. He claims, "No jobs out there." He keeps sitting in his house and wonders, "How am I going to pay the mortgage?" He assumes he won't find a job and doesn't bother to look for one other than to occasionally glance at an online job site that seems to confirm his worst thoughts.

What's John doing? The bad news media and other poor souls wallowing in their misfortune swallow John up like quicksand.

BE A PART OF THE SOLUTION — ALWAYS!

Be a part of the solution not the problem. If you, like John, dwell on negative beliefs and do absolutely nothing to change your situation, you are being part of the problem. In fact, *you* are the problem. When you decide to plan for change; to plan to actively take positive steps toward your desired vision; to pursue your vision with dogged determination, passion and commitment; to believe you will receive your wishes and live your dreams; and persist at doing those things that move you not just toward but into your vision, then you will one day wake up and know you've arrived. You will not just say, "I intend to start a coaching business," you will tell people you are a life coach and *soon you will have clients galore.* Not just say I intend to get a job, you find a job by doing all that is necessary to find one. You will not just say I want to find my soul mate, you find a soul mate by going out and meeting new people *in the right places.* But before you take action, you must KNOW what it is you want. What kind of work do you enjoy doing? What qualities define your soul mate? KNOW what you want!

Your plan for resilience to achieve your vision starts with small action steps. It starts with a list of what you will actively do to pursue your vision. I suggest you make a list of five action steps you will take toward your goals each day — not only when the going is easy, but also (and especially) when the going gets tough. I have very specific actions I take when I start to feel distracted, angry or down. When I feel my mind slip into old habits and ways of thinking, My "how to" stay the course goes like this:

- If a barrier gets in my way, I avoid overwhelming feelings of sadness and depression by clearing my mind — I clear out the fear. Often, the best way to do this is by feeling whatever feelings I'm having (rather than "stuffing" them), reasoning with and examining them, and then moving on.
- I meditate and focus on my vision. I see what I want to accomplish. I visualize my goals as if they have already taken place.
- If I get a piece of news I don't like, I don't automatically assume the worst-case scenario. I don't shed negative light on the news. I accept what is and think about solutions … here's the situation; what can I do about it? How do I get through, over, under or around what may seem like an insurmountable barrier or obstacle.
- Then I realize that nothing is really an obstacle but merely a distraction. When I understand the situation, then I am not distracted (or intimidated) by it. I simply face it — take it out, look at it for what it really is, shrug and throw it back. Done! Move on.
- I clear my head. Then I consider what is next? How do I take action? What do I do to make it different? Nothing deters or distracts — at least not for very long. I just get creative. I find ways to

move forward with a clear head and a sound mind and body.

- Finally, I apply my never-ending mantra, "It will be OK!" "It IS OK!" You know what? It always is! Just know that in your heart and soul.

If you assume control over your thinking and empower yourself with positive action steps to clear out the gunk, you will retrain your mind toward positivity. You will revolutionize and transform your self-defeating behaviors almost effortlessly. It might seem difficult at first. You most probably will not change the behaviors all at once. It takes practice; one moment at a time. You might start to see and feel your new vision, but deal with a distracting moment. Soon, as you build your new habits into a brand-new value system of action (rather than reaction), you will become a person filled with joy and happiness. You will move into your vision and enjoy the rewards. You will be healthier and happier — no doubt! For how can a person so energized by his or her world, so filled with joy, and so grateful for it all not be happy? Not want to live and love and enjoy?

I can tell you with total certainty that reprogramming your mind, body and spirit to see the beauty, abundance and possibility that surround you every day will transform you. You will without reservation or doubt learn the power of resilience and, in fact, you will simply be on a higher plain of living where the need for resilience isn't a lesson to be learned anymore; it is simply a way of being.

Next, I'm going to teach you milestones and confirmations that you're on the right path.

Chapter Four

*What Do Successful People Do?
How Can YOU Do it?*

"Spiritual freedom comes from participating in the moment-by-moment flow of life, not by getting things to be just right once and for all."
— SUSAN CAMPBELL, RELATIONSHIP COACH

Did you know that the Great Depression produced more millionaires than any other time in our nation's history? During the worst economic downturn our country experienced, people continued to be successful. How is that even possible, you wonder? Well, habits and attitudes of success transcend and buck the obvious economic trends. People who possess these habits and attitudes will thrive no matter what and despite what is happening in the world at large. Now mind you, success is much more than material wealth. Some people feel incredibly successful just living a happy, healthy life. You don't have to pursue millionaire status to be successful, but let's be real — money provides many of the comforts of life, not to mention all the good you can do with it (you can reach a lot further than your physical self when you have the financial means). So we don't want to downplay financial wealth. Actually, I would like to quote Jim Rohn here and challenge you to: "Set a goal to become a millionaire for what it will make of you to reach it." You see, there is so much more to becoming a millionaire than a big bank account. Success and wealth *include,* but are not limited to, finances; it's very important to be clear on this!

A BIG part of evaluating your journey to success, no matter what goes on around you in the external world, is looking inward first. You have goals to reach and a vision to create, so only YOU can make it happen; and here's how:

Step one: Get real with yourself and figure out your strengths and weaknesses — understand what propels you forward and what holds you back from achieving your vision. You must believe that you can pursue any vision you have imagined, and then take action; this is why you need to look candidly at where you've been, where you are, and where you want to go. Learn from your past mistakes and successes (where you've been); figure out exactly where you are in life (all aspects: physically, spiritually, financially, etc.); and map out the rest of your journey forward (not limited by your past or present). Dare to dream and build your vision! The get-real part requires an honest, clear and direct self-assessment. Your perception of yourself needs to be pulled out, examined, transformed and returned to its proper place. "Truth telling time" means looking inside, examining past behavior; assessing skills, strengths and talents; and then faithfully figuring out how to transform and move forward.

I want you to understand — *you can't go forward without an honest assessment.* Otherwise you end up repeating the same patterns and mistakes and thinking the same thoughts that hold you back. An honest assessment of you (your authentic self) requires an evaluation of all things that have come to pass. It means you quit lying to yourself. I will say this over and over again. I am not your judge or jury, so I'm not here to drag your character through the mud. I am here only to assist you in this personal journey. You don't have to "confess" anything to anyone to make this change. Your only confession needs to be to you. You have to look at everything about "you" objectively — but most importantly with integrity and honesty. You may find this self-assessment really hard, at first, but allow the process to take place. We ALL have our battles to fight; the good news is they're not as hard as they seem, and the reward is amazing! *Refer to the assessment on my website (www.DreamPlanAchieve.com). You may also want to take advantage of a free consultation with me.*

Ideas that we've been fed from family, friends and society can cloud our perception of ourselves. Other people's ideas and opinions of you — I want to emphasize here — are not YOU! Big and important message here: You are *NOT the sum total of other people's projections onto you.* You may find it really difficult to overcome these superimposed, external opinions and judgments you've been spoon-fed by your uninvited peanut gallery; but here is where it all changes … beginning today, right now! You do NOT need to define yourself by anything other than your own criteria. And set those criteria to the dreamiest, most picturesque level you can ever imagine. The time is ripe for transformation, but don't attempt to try it without changing how you think about yourself, which leads to a discussion about your "self" talk or what I refer to as "smack talk" (the negative tracks in your mind).

SUCCESSFUL PEOPLE DON'T USE NEGATIVE SELF TALK

One thing I can assure you, the athlete with the gold medal did not say to him or herself, "I cannot do it." Can you imagine an athlete saying something that uninspired? In fact, a good bet suggests that winners separate themselves from losers by their attitudes. It's unthinkable that a "winner" or a successful person sits around before the big race and says, "I'm never going to make it." Winners are like the good old train in the children's story that says, "I think I can, I think I can, I think I can," except that they KNOW they can (through daily practice of positive thinking!). They do not say, "Oh darn that recession. Now I can count on being unemployed. Go figure, I can never get ahead; I'm a loser, might as well admit it! I'm on my way out. I can't control the economy; can't control my boss; there's just nothing I can do that will get me out of this rut I live in — this is my lot in life. It's so unfair!"

If you're the type of person who talks that way to yourself, then you should pay close attention. Winners don't have time for negative talk; they are too busy figuring out how to win! They are positive thinkers and take action with the "I-know-I-can" message playing in their heads. An important reason why you must change negative "smack talk" is because *what you think about, you will definitely attract* (every study of the Laws of

Attraction confirms this). If you have a lot of negative thoughts about yourself, you pull in more of the same old, same old. So you must drill down to the inner core of your "smack talk" and zap it out of existence ... quit undermining yourself!

Now you may be thinking, "Who cares? No one else hears it but me. Besides, who am I kidding ... I'm no good; all this 'woo-woo, hoorah' talk is a bunch of bologna." Really? Don't be so sure. Negative inner talk has this interesting way of creeping or "seeping" into your very soul. We already mentioned that your thoughts betray you; they lie to you all the time! You must talk back ... reason with them, don't just accept them at face value. Remember, *What you think about, you attract.* I'm going to say that over and over again. If you think you're ugly then you probably dress, talk and act ugly. If you think you're handsome and smart, you probably dress, talk and act smart. The list goes on. So stop talking smack to *yourself!* If you feel completely lost and don't know how to shut down the smack talk, try these three simple steps:

#1: Start catching it. Notice and listen closely. Those of you saying right now, "I don't have a negative voice in my head" ... well, you just heard the voice! I am smiling right now at you.

#2: Stop saying it to yourself. You can literally rein in your mind. It's when you let that "little voice" drone on and on, unchecked, that the "seepage" occurs.

#3: Turn a negative into a positive. Replace the negative with the positive. I am smart. I am handsome. I am beautiful. I am powerful. I am warm and friendly. I am … (positive word). Some people call these affirmations. Some coaches often suggest you say these affirmations to yourself in the mirror. Affirmations don't have to be said in front of the mirror. You just need to say them over and over again to replace negative tracks. Do whatever works for YOU ... you can start with recommendations from me and others, but eventually you need to tailor everything to fit YOU — everything POSITIVE, that is.

I don't want to give you platitudes on negative self-talk. You know that hearing and *recognizing* your own negative self-talk will challenge you. You may feel so completely, miserably uncomfortable, even just drilling down into the negative well. Just know that it takes baby steps to accomplish great things. So just get started; dive right in there. Taking small, engaging gestures toward opening the can of writhing, ugly worms will cause you pain — great pain at times. You won't get warm-and-fuzzy feelings. In fact, you may want to crumble before you crawl. So, I'm going to help you ease the pain. Just start with a simple awareness — "hear" the voice and understand what it keeps saying. If you feel like you can't control the voice, don't struggle; just stop for a minute, BREATHE (seriously, breathe), reason with this voice, feel what you feel, then think of and meditate on positive things — and repeat positive affirmations over and over again (see #3 above). Next time you hear the voice, say "Yes, I heard you, but it's not true." Then replace the negative words with their polar opposite. OK, simple, direct exercises. I said simple, but not necessarily easy in the beginning — so practice and keep practicing until you get it right, and then practice some more!

I want to emphasize that this work (and believe me it's hard work), will not happen overnight. In fact, none of the "wisdom" I impart in this book happens overnight (believe me; I know from personal experience). Remind yourself of these three (well, three and one-half) simple words every day: *It's a process.* My best advice is: don't bail out on your process. Part of being successful requires you to stay the course, keep your vision front and center, and keep moving toward your goal — step by step.

LOOSEN THOSE FIXED THOUGHTS

Fixed thoughts cause ongoing harm, because the person who has them may have become so used to them and so oblivious that she/he has no realization these thoughts even exist. In fact, fixed negative thoughts fall under the radar because they become almost a part of your family's DNA — and I don't mean that which makes up our physical body chemistry. Most families have habits and common belief systems passed down from generation to generation. Many people do certain things simply because "this is how we do it around here (in our family; our town; our country ...)." Or because "this is how we've always done things." When you think about it, does this "reasoning" make sense? It's not even "reasoning," is it? When you reason with someone or something, you must use one of your intellectual faculties ... you must get all the facts! (I discuss the Six Intellectual Faculties in detail in my workbook *"MIND Your Wellness."*)

Fixed behaviors and beliefs can go on and on without question or consideration as to whether or not they hurt or thwart the people involved. Let's give the extreme example of a group we'll call "the-cup-is-half-empty thinkers." Some families have a matriarch or patriarch who is a negative thinker. They say and behave in ways that show their negativity to their children. They criticize, complain and condemn somebody and/or something every single day. Their negative behavior is a part of their daily routine much like a bowl of "Depressing-Os" for breakfast. Something bad happens, negative people seize on it, "Of course, that is reality. Life sucks." They are unable to see good in most situations. They put their children down rather than act supportive, upbeat and hopeful. They tell Sally she needs a new hairstyle and pick at her clothes, makeup and her overall look. They tell her she's stupid when she gets one C, yet the rest of her grades are As and Bs. They see little to no good in the world — and can complain about the happiest place on Earth! This negative behavior is picked up and applied by their children and their children's children, etc. Now, not everyone in the family will subscribe to the negative behavior. Those who don't must overcome the deeply engrained tracks laid down in their minds (by well-meaning people). They must be conscious seekers of change and growth. They must become self aware and take 100-percent responsibility for their lives — because this deeply engrained way of thinking and being is very difficult to overcome ... but not impossible. As a matter of fact, once one takes charge of one's own life and begins this amazing process, one will find freedom — priceless freedom!

Let me give you another example. A common story told by counselors is the one about the ham and the baking pan. A woman used to take a ham and cut off the ends (good meat) to make it square. Why would you cut off the good meat just to make a ham square? It turns out that her mother cut the ham in a square and her mother's mother cut the ham the same way. Why did the grandmother cut the ham in a square? Back at the turn of the century, they didn't have a baking pan the size of a full cut of ham; hence, she had to cut her ham in that shape to fit it in the pan. Since that time — even with different pan sizes available — no one had ever questioned why. It was just what you did when you cook a ham. What an odd and totally wasteful "family tradition," but it just shows you how families (and society as a whole) inadvertently develop fixed ideas about things, and then pass them down to generation after generation. Somewhere along the way, one important detail gets forgotten or left out, but the idea keeps going on and on — just because — that is, until someone decides to ask why and keep asking until he/she gets a valid answer.

What are your fixed ideas? Whether inherited from years of family traditions or acquired through no question on your part about their validity or impact on your life and your ability to be successful, you have fixed ideas — we all have these ideas. So don't worry, you're not alone! What matters most as you begin your transformation is your ability to identify those fixed thoughts. Some people's fixed thoughts become their rationale for not doing something they would really love to do — their "excuses" for avoiding certain situations that stretch them beyond their current "comfort" zones.

Have you ever noticed that some families produce generations of entrepreneurs or teachers or doctors? Their family has embraced a certain way of thinking about that profession and engenders and promotes their family members' involvement. A friend's husband comes from a family where all of the men own and operate their own businesses. In that family, the entrepreneurial spirit is alive and well. They embrace all of the things that might scare a family of government workers. To them, taking a risk is a good thing! A steady paycheck is a foreign idea; independence matters; and freedom is to be continually sought after and attained. Meanwhile, the family of government workers eschews all of those beliefs and embraces "security," steady paychecks and promotions up the bureaucratic ladder as a measure of success. The entrepreneurial family would grimace at the confines of a "secure" job and vice versa. What makes these two families so different? Nothing, except they have different fixed thoughts about their careers. I knew a fellow that worked for the federal government for 40 years and every time his son brought up going independent, he steered him off the thought by focusing on "fear-based" ideas he so openly embraced (like how risky it would be … and what would he do without the "benefits" package, etc.). Rather than encouraging his son, who was very unhappy working in the government environment, to go after what he wanted, he preaches on the "great benefits" of having a "steady" job and "talks some sense into his head." What's really sad is the fact that this father thinks he's doing his son a favor by teaching him to be "realistic." I know, I used a LOT of quotation marks … I just want to make sure I'm communicating that this perceived wisdom may not be the truth for everyone.

Part of your unhappiness and inability to become successful probably involves these kinds of fixed thoughts and beliefs. You have been so trained to believe a certain way about something — anything — that you can no longer identify what holds you back. You feel completely trapped in your own belief system. You don't know what keeps you stuck and you don't know how to figure it out or where to begin to move past it. So how do you figure out what keeps your feet stuck in the fixed-thoughts mud? My best advice is this: open your heart to all possibilities. If you have become a corporate drone and want nothing more than to get out and on your own, ask yourself, "What's stopping me? Why? And, why not?"

Why not start a business?

Why not get married to the partner of your dreams?

Why not take a trip to Italy?

Why not write a book?

Why not become a public speaker?

Why not make good money every day?

Why not? And then fill in the blank. I can assure you that answer contains your fixed thought. You're falling off your chair. No way! It can't be that easy! Oh yes, it can. Those fixed thoughts exist under the why-not answers. If you honestly and authentically write down even your knee-jerk response, there you go. You're probably blown away saying, "That can't be." Yes, friends, the "why not" is a powerful, revealing tool to unhinge deeply rooted beliefs that hold you back from living your full potential.

So we know that negative fixed thoughts and behaviors hold you back. Self-defeating behaviors are pretty insidious monsters, too. These behaviors need to stop before you can get on the "how" road to success. Self-defeating behaviors are the worst roadblocks, because you often can't see them as clearly as you must. Self-defeating behaviors are often deeply engrained habits that become our mental safety nets. These habits don't save you though, they enslave you!

You understand that when you don't grab hold and take over the helm of your life, you become a "slave" to habit — a bystander in your own life (an extra in your own movie). People tend to give away their personal power to these habits that hold them back. If you're reading this book right now hoping to achieve success, then you have made a powerful first step. You feel ready to move on and get unstuck and pursue your success with all of your might. You feel ready to face whatever facts you have to face, make a change, and grow and learn the beauty and art of "how" to be a success.

You're taking a step to get out of the robotic state of the masses and on with the bigger things of life. I know how you feel as you become consumed in the thoughts of "how" to move on when you feel so stuck. You have no idea how your story will turn out; I promise — no I guarantee — that the very fact that you feel ready to move, means you've come face to face with the realization that you, like me, are ready to become your own hero.

So taking the next steps and learning how to change old patterns of behavior and ways of thinking (so that you can find new ways of being positive) means going back to your answers to the big question: "Why not?" Why not travel to Europe? Answer: I can't afford it. Flip the negative over. Like I mentioned earlier, Wayne Dyer said it best, "We can afford anything we want." (A little side note: This statement used to offend me — I would think to myself, it's easy for "you rich people" to make such ignorant statements … what do you know about affording things? You can get whatever you want, whenever you want; how dare you judge me and say that I can afford anything I want like I'm just wasteful and stupid about finances? Do you see the hypocrisy in this … I mean MY hypocrisy? I am judging them while accusing them of judging me! Stay with me, keep your mind open, and believe me, this process works!

So put the negative of "I can't afford it" through positive, rose-colored glasses that suggest abundance and possibility: God wants us all to live in abundance; he doesn't want us to deprive ourselves. God doesn't want to punish, judge or cast us into harsh poverty and keep beauty and love from us. We might think that deprivation and lack of abundance are universal truths when, in fact, abundance, overflow and wealth provide the real backdrop to our lives. Nothing in the world really suggests otherwise. Consider that everything we could ever need exists and will always exist for us. *We just have to take action to first understand, and then grab hold and believe.* Believe God means abundance to be ours. Believe we deserve abundance. Believe we shall have abundance. And then with love and gratitude, accept it and say thank you.

Chapter Five

The Whole World Has Changed — Learn to Live the New Normal

"Do not make the recession your obsession, just remember to forget it and you'll be OK."
— MINA TADROS

Let's say for one moment you're not going to look at or count on some fluke in the economy to determine your future and open new opportunities. Let's instead suggest you're going to rely on your own vision and plans to move forward. And let's also suggest you have adjusted your attitude, and you're ready to go for your dreams. In fact, what you are going to do is look inward and rely on your own ability to make your life happen.

In today's economic world — full of unpleasant and some very pleasant changes (depending on how you look at it) — you face only the obstacles you put in your own way. This economic downfall came at an interesting kind of intersection in the world. Many adults were already facing a kind of spiritual bankruptcy that was forcing a question of quality of life versus quantity in life (meaning materialism). At the same time, you had the economy fall on its face; but interestingly enough the convergence of this angst combined with the reality of market sectors (either in decline or disappearing altogether) produced a new generation of entrepreneurs.

So let's pull back for a second to help you understand what we're saying. Despite the economic hardship clearly plaguing many Americans, a segment of this group, on their own and outside of what appeared to be scary future prospects, left corporate or a job or whatever … to start companies. Case study after case study reveals entrepreneurs who will confess with much enthusiasm that they actually left their corporate job with no threat of being laid off whatsoever. They left a perfectly good and often high-paying job to start their own businesses or to achieve some sort of a dream. Many of you out there may believe these folks were either foolish or brave; however, when asked, these entrepreneurs don't feel either of those notions about their exits. In fact, these people's corporate/job-exit strategies were not predicated on anything other than an urgent desire to reach a dream or improve the quality of their lives. And it is this scenario that tells a much deeper story about this generation's feelings about the person they want to be in the world, how they want to live, and what legacy they want to leave behind. So while it may seem incomprehensible that anyone would leave a six-figure, secure position in this economy, it happens every day as more and more people realize that a real spiritual evolution is taking place — not just a financial downfall that will stabilize and go back up at some point (and maybe it already has by the time you pick up this book).

Now some people are following their dreams because the recession forced a kind of self and spiritual reckoning — perhaps without the recession's push, they might have stayed put. Yet at the same time, this doesn't explain why new entrepreneurs emerged of their own volitions during these difficult times; but a whole picture can be drawn if you examine commonalities amongst the two groups — because a common theme exists.

GENERATION "V"

Whether pushed out or voluntarily making a change, many people decided not to jump back on the job train so they can pursue a dream — one that has very little to do with materialism (although material wealth is a by-product of the change). A new generation we'll call Generation V (V for values) has arisen. Generation V is a unique group of people who felt that their often material-driven lives had come to a standstill in terms of happiness. Financial success had become comparable to a sugar-free cupcake — looks pretty on the outside but tastes a bit off. Some highly successful people looked at their bank accounts and then back on their lives only to feel a huge chasm — they felt, well, BLAH! A big bank account didn't really mean anything to them. It's much like what the character Lestat says in the movie *Interview with the Vampire,* "Life has no meaning anymore, does it? The wine has no taste, food sickens you, and there seems no reason for any of it."

Those feelings reflect the disenfranchisement of Generation V — most of whom have come to realize the need for change. Generation V has embraced the idea that personal values and quality of life trump material success or even job security. Generation V doesn't embrace the idea that a Mercedes in your driveway says anything special or important about you other than you have financial success (maybe!). Great — and again, we have nothing against financial wealth; but what Generation V values far more than a Mercedes and/or financial success is true freedom — freedom to pursue a dream, travel, spend leisure time with family, and the ability to live a life not driven by the constraints of rules determined by a bureaucracy or invisible big brother. Generation V comprises a new cohort of entrepreneurs, artists, life coaches, authors, writers, designers, and other free agents who don't commute, punch a card or report to anyone. Generation V would much rather take a trip to the South of France or work from their homes to be with their children than own a Mercedes or a mansion on the hill. Generation V tends to want power and control over how and when they work versus just the *ability to work.* And mind you, Generation V often works as hard or even harder than the average person (but they ENJOY their work). So, this lifestyle choice — and it's definitely about lifestyle — has very little to do with a lack of desire to work.

Generation V pursues those avenues that enable them to have a better quality of life. They are driven and motivated by what they feel passionate about. They need to have a sense of purpose. And most importantly they are committed to that passion and purpose and absolutely nothing gets in their way of this pursuit. They do not let the outer world determine for them what they can or cannot do as long as they have their desire to pursue their passion square in their line of sight. They will apply what we described in the last two chapters — the power of positivity — to be their guide and generally block out bad, negative information that might pollute how they think. They know everything we've discussed to date, and they apply it. But above all else, Generation V's biggest concern is about living their values.

Generation V has often learned the hard way that they don't want their entire lives stolen by a demanding job or corporate tract that takes them away from their families (sometimes 14 hours a day) and puts them on the road for weeks on end. Generation V values their ability to be present and active parents or to be able to help *their* parents, siblings and friends. They are not interested in a disconnected lifestyle that perhaps pays high salaries or produces huge profits, while destroying their family life and their own wellbeing.

Generation V truly puts personal life first. It's very, very important for those of you who feel the angst we've described — the desire for freedom and independence — to know that you are not alone. You simply subscribe to the values of this generation. You should also know that thousands of other people like you will change the landscape of the business and professional world — and already have made a considerable impact.

Did you know that more women than men are currently becoming entrepreneurs in this recession? No study needs to be conducted to provide the obvious answer as to why! Thousands of women have discovered that they have the passion, prowess, skill and determination to live their dreams. Many of these women are also mothers who have put a stake in their home offices versus continue to try and juggle careers and family. These women of Generation V want to see the first steps of toddlers; they want to be home to pick up school-age children; they want to take time off in the middle of the day to attend soccer games; but at the same time, they don't wish to give up fulfilling dreams and career wishes.

Highly successful, independent men and women shape the new economic world we live in. They are out there. They are making their own way. They value things differently than workers who came before them. They want more than a great car, house, boat and other toys. They chase their dreams. They have a completely different view about how they want to live and BE. They are often very spiritually motivated. They care about being happy and having a fulfilling personal life. If you are reading this and you possess those traits, then you are part of Generation V; if you're in business and reading this, be aware that this is the next generation and understand how this generation thinks and behaves; and finally if you made a mental note that you feel like Generation V and you're sitting somewhere like a cubicle in corporate ... well, keep reading this book to help you get yourself unstuck — that is, if you have not already figured it out.

Chapter Six

Tips, Tricks and 10 Tools for Success

"The people who get on in this world
are the people who get up and look for the
circumstances they want
and if they can't find them, make them."
— GEORGE BERNARD SHAW

OK, you've come this far in the book. You've considered and maybe even taken my advice. You may start feeling more confident and assured as you make changes and shifts in your outlook. You're thinking positive, monitoring the internal negative talk, meditating on good things, changing those old sound tracks, avoiding excuses that keep you stuck, and benefiting from the rewards that come from applying the Laws of Attraction to manifest a new life. You've changed your mental outlook, created a spectacular vision that motivates and suits you, and you have actually taken action to get up and on with it. You have the principles of resilience as your own manifesto for better living. You've honed in on who you want to be in the world — and it all feels great.

You feel like a rock star and bask in the glow of newfound self confidence and resilience, and then ... a slow feeling creeps up and nags at you. A dark feeling you can't shake. You start questioning and asking yourself, "Now that I have a new vision and a plan, how do I stay on course? How do I know that I'm really on course at all?" Questions like these plant seeds of doubt. You may begin to waffle. Fear may creep back in out of nowhere. Why do you feel afraid and nervous when things appear to be nicely moving forward?

First, change puts most people out of their comfort zones. They're not used to living a life where the ups keep going up and the downs become mere blimps on their radars. Folks — especially those addicted to drama — may find something feels off-kilter. They start waiting like an expectant parent for a big event that never seems to come. Rather than enjoy the forward motion, these folks become vigilant as they wait for the next disaster to hit — or better yet they actively seek an "emotional drug pusher" to help create an explosive situation guaranteed to push them spiraling right back down to their "comfort (miserable) zone."

So, here is something you need to know right away. Your new outlook will become an everyday way of living — or the new normal. Your new normal requires constant measuring, evaluating and more importantly staying in the right mindset — and if you think that sounds pretty straightforward you are wrong. You may fall into autopilot at any second and quit keeping your eye on your vision. You may give in to fear and anxiety. Something may set you off. You may just have an off day. It happens — and it's OK. What you need to do is reflect and see the milestones you've worked toward. Acknowledge the momentum and forward march toward your goals. You can get nervous and feel anxious, but the key to open the door requires you to step back and celebrate the signposts and recognize you're on track. Simply understand the process and that understanding will get you through the tough times.

I've personally experienced what it feels like to transform my personal outlook. I am a resilient woman, but like everyone else, I have my ups and downs. When things seem to be on the downside versus the upside, I really examine where I'm coming from in my outlook. Am I being motivated by fear and anxiety? If that's the case, I look at it and ask myself, "What am I afraid of?" I've also learned to manage the setbacks and look at them differently. What you should do, though, is pay attention to the accomplishments that have taken you toward your vision. Reward yourself and see that all of these wonderful incremental changes continually pay off. You may or may not experience 100-percent transformation overnight; but you must acknowledge for yourself (don't look outside of yourself for positive reinforcement) how you've experienced these changes and how good it feels. When I take time out to reflect on how far I've personally come in my own journey, it helps me better cope with the difficult times. I can also use my past successes to correct my course and keep from taking a turn backward … then shift my attention to the bigger picture. I continually use the Laws of Attraction and positive thinking to bring more good things into my life. I visualize outcomes I want to experience and try to avoid falling into mental traps where repetitive negative thoughts make me feel scared and depressed. Focus on the positive milestones and keep your attention away from negative "poor-me" moments where you feel sorry for yourself — a place where you let fear and depression get back in the driver's seat.

A lot of people in this economy have allowed the constant messages from the media and the world at large to drive fear into their hearts. They've lost sight of their focus. They listen to and allow the garbage to seep in — even when they KNOW they must keep their eyes straight ahead. They opt not to focus on their milestones and successes, but "assume" that negative news is going to make up their realities. Unfortunately, this route seems to be the easier one to take — I say "seems" because far from being "easier," this route leads to absolute disaster. If you're one of millions who lost their jobs, know this important message: you can go home, switch on the TV, and be spoon fed more bad news ... OR you can create a vision and move toward it. Every positive step you acknowledge will lead to another; soon you will have a landslide of positive moments that accumulate into one big triumphant life.

MILESTONE MEASUREMENTS

Now you may ask, "How do I know when I've hit a milestone?" When you apply the Laws of Attraction, change your outlook, and notice how you act and feel about situations, you hit milestones almost instantly — because these milestones are little, incremental accomplishments that move you forward in the direction of your goal. You just have to believe you've hit them, even though you may not see monumental results, *yet* ("yet" being the key word here). Let me give you an example. I have this friend we'll call "Henry" who lost his high-powered executive position with a major technology company. We talked a few times, and he was initially all about the "poor-me" stuff. He felt depressed and didn't know how he was going to start over. A few conversations later, he pulled it together. He started to visualize his ideal job. Next, he started networking. He got a few leads, but he still hadn't gotten a firm interview. What did Henry decide to do? He threw in the towel and got really depressed again and fell right back into the "poor-me" stuff.

What's wrong here? Why is Henry back to the recliner, eating Ring-Dings, and watching mind-numbing TV? Why isn't he sitting in a big office with a view? Maybe you're thinking (as he might be), "Hey! It didn't work out." He doesn't have a job, does he? Henry's story might even sound pretty familiar — maybe you're a Henry. Henry blames the economy. He doesn't believe any jobs exist (after all, it's all over the "bad" news — there are no jobs out there). He just can't find one; therefore, the story must be true, he rationalizes. All that mind-numbing TV tells him so every day.

What has Henry done wrong? First, he got off on the right foot. He got out and started networking.

He got some leads. He felt excited. He could see his end goal in sight; then no interviews materialized. No offers. Still without a job, Henry failed to acknowledge his milestones. He didn't see that he had resiliently overcome the lure to stay stuck in a recliner — all sad and depressed and hopeless. He had gone out and met some great folks. He had generated some leads. Somehow all that positive action got buried in the miry clay of perceived failure and all the negative connotations that go with "failure." He didn't celebrate the milestones; he *chose* to wallow in "failure."

What Henry and everyone else in a similar situation needs to realize is this: it takes *action* to grow, change and attain success — sustained *action.* When you start to make things happen, you can't expect smooth sailing all the way; you also cannot afford to stop the minute you hit a little bump in the road. Would you rather tear through your fear and anxiety or fall backward into a deep, dark void of endless disappointments? Henry failed to acknowledge the wonder of each new opportunity. He focused only on the negative — the phone didn't ring. He didn't get a job interview. He didn't get hired. Negative, negative, negative! What if the next step Henry took led him to his dream job? As Napoleon Hill tells the story in his book "Think and Grow Rich," "Don't stop three feet from gold! Your success is waiting for you around the corner." Will you stop and give up? Or will you turn that corner? Are you going to stop — give up — three feet from gold? Stay focused on your ultimate goal; give up the negative thoughts and disappointments; and celebrate the positive actions you take every day until one day (sooner than later) you hit the big vein of gold!

PERSIST AND PERSEVERE — EVERY SINGLE DAY

What's the number one rule in resilience? *You must persist and persevere!* Yes, persistence and perseverance — just don't give up; keep trying; keep going — and you WILL arrive. I know that sounds kind of obvious and maybe too simple, but it works, every time! So keep celebrating and acknowledging the milestones. Focus on what is rather than what is not; be grateful for what you have rather than worry about what you do not have. Each milestone builds to the next and the next — and when you stay the course and you keep going and celebrating each step, you soon arrive at the vision — YOUR vision. This is the "icing on the cake" — it feels fantastic!

Let me give you another example. I know this woman we'll call "Melinda." Right in the middle of this so-called economic crisis, Melinda decided she no longer wanted to deal with her one-hour commute and lack of time with her family (which, of course, strained her marriage). She wanted to seek a better quality of life. She always wanted to start a business, so she decided one day she was just going to do it. She quit her six-figure income job (right in the firestorm of layoffs) and started her marketing company. Two weeks before her last day of work, she already had checks waiting for her. She had started picking up side business about a month before her departure. She prepared for the transition. She networked and picked up business. She joined new organizations. She met prospective business clients and pursued opportunities. Her transition from corporate to business owner never hiccupped.

Why is Melinda different from Henry? Melinda does not allow anything or anybody to depress her, cause her fear, or dissuade her from her vision. She goes after what she wants and takes action and, most importantly, celebrates each new win. She thanks God for each new day; for not having to commute; for enjoying extra time with her family. She stays positive every day. Yes, of course she has bad days just like everybody else, but she just refuses to dwell on them. Her time and life are too valuable to waste on guilt and regret. She doesn't feel bitter about anything. She simply acknowledges, "Hey, I'm having a bad day;

what's the lesson/opportunity in it?" end of story. No wallowing. No pity parties. No whining. Simply living and enjoying every moment of life she's blessed with.

Melinda sees every moment as precious — and each new milestone as amazing. She stays focused and on course. Incidentally, Melinda's company is now a half-million dollar company — in less than a year AND in *this* economy! Melinda persists and perseveres. She gets it. She moves with the current and follows her passions. She doesn't waver — ever! Now you doubters may groan, "Oh, but she's just lucky!" Are you sure that's all she is ... lucky? Melinda's journey has absolutely nothing to do with luck! Let me continue and help you understand. (Incidentally, luck isn't winning the lottery ticket — someone's got to! Luck would be winning the lottery without buying a ticket!)

A WHOLE OTHER ZONE

Why is Melinda successful when millions of other people are not? First and foremost, Melinda followed her passion, crafted a vision to realize her passion (dreamed, planned and achieved). She now feels absolutely amazing about every step she takes to pursue her passion. She hangs in there when necessary by focusing on what's working and on her overall plans — the BIG picture. She doesn't allow negative distractions to get in her way. She persists and perseveres. *When you follow your passion and persist with such solid certainty that your vision will be attained, no one and nothing can knock you down.* You know who you are and where you're going. Let me repeat: *Know who you are and where you're going.* Your vision requires complete and utter certainty that it can be attained. You can do it — if only through rock-solid, hard-core persistence and perseverance. Does any of that sound like it is related to luck or coincidence? Now let me take it a step further.

You hear about athletes all the time who win gold medals. They talk about being focused and "in the zone." If you don't know what "the zone" is, let me tell you. The zone is that passionate, perfect focus that blocks out all distractions. When we get in the zone, we lose track of time and space. We're completely immersed in something that is almost pure energy — and it's a beautiful, beautiful thing. Living in the zone transcends time, space and place. You become this energetic force of pure positive light that merges with the universe. You are completely focused on what you're doing and know deep within you — without doubt or reservation — that you can do it and will do it. If you've never experienced that complete and utter plugging into the universe, you have missed something so special and so beyond your physical mind and body. When you exist in that place, your celebration of the milestones becomes one big enlightened realization that all things are not just possible but are already happening every second and moment of every day.

Falling out of the zone becomes this kind of irritating moment. It's like a zap of light in a dark room. You squint and holler, "Turn off that light!" I know this sounds absolutely nuts … crazy! But I promise you, when you have risen so far above the daily drone meant only to pull you out of your spirit and distract you from your vision, you will truly be bathed in complete magic. The more you embrace and celebrate every moment and hug the achievements as they come (in whatever increments), the more you will experience absolutely amazing, magical and just incredible things happen every day of your life. Pure jubilance and happiness will become the norm — the rest will fall to the wayside.

I pledge this to be true. I live it every day. I am amazed and grateful for what God gives me. I am overwhelmed and joyful over every moment of life. I am just blown away. How can it get better? Yet it gets better! More fantastic events and people come into my life. More wonder and magic happen. And always … always (hear this) *I thank God for all of it!* You know what else? When you get to that place of euphoria, it is unreal how hard it becomes to actually be angry, depressed or sad … ever. I know many of you don't believe me. You're thinking, "Nobody's that happy!" Yet I am a walking, talking example of how what I explained is possible — it is real for me; it can be for you too. You just have to believe and go for it!

CELEBRATE THE SMALL STUFF

Sometimes as you begin your walk in resilience, you may feel like nothing has changed — or nothing has changed dramatically enough. Maybe you were expecting to visualize your new life, take action to make it happen, and all will be well; but three months later you begin to feel like you're no closer than you were when you started. You may feel disappointed that the changes you're experiencing don't seem big enough. You may feel impatient, frustrated or even discouraged. Maybe all of the tips I've shared seem just like a bunch of nonsense. At this point in your journey it's time to stop, evaluate your progress, focus on the FACTS, and fully embrace the *small* changes. Don't give up on your dream so easily; enjoy the journey!

Each baby step puts you just that much closer to your vision. Sometimes during this journey, you will make dramatic leaps and other times you will have inched along and perhaps never realized just how far all that "inching" took you. No matter what the changes, you will find it valuable and inspiring when you stop and "smell the 'real' little changes" — the milestones. I want to emphasize the importance of taking these moments to recognize the smaller stuff. Your ability to identify the positive forward motion — no matter how small — will not only confirm but affirm just how far you've come, and perhaps reboot your mental outlook, which may have taken a downward slide.

Even the most successful people stumble when something comes unexpectedly along to dampen their spirits and propel them spiraling into a dark place, they quickly lose sight of everything great in their lives. No matter what happens, you will need the ability to stop and not just celebrate but recognize you deserve a pat on the back. You're making great strides. You're resilient now. You must become objective and notice everything changing. Maybe, since starting your own business, you've quit waking up in the morning dreading the day. Maybe your business isn't quite thriving, but you're at least re-energized about it. Maybe you've finally met a prospective mate and you have someone to go to dinner with on Friday night. You're not alone and you're sharing intimacy. Doesn't it feel great? Or you finally started tucking away money to take your vacation to Italy. You have $500 when you had none just three months ago.

You've empowered yourself. You've taken charge. You've focused on what you want. You go for abundance and positivity. At this point, you need to stop and acknowledge all that. You need to smile and appreciate you've come this far. You need to thank God for where you are today ... *because yesterday is gone and tomorrow hasn't come yet.* All you have is this particular moment — this second in time, so why not appreciate what you've got and how far you've come? Why not celebrate and honor your progress? You deserve it! Here comes the crux of the matter ... you need to give yourself the kudos, because expecting others to do it for you won't cut it. You will face daily challenges that can derail your progress at any time, so it's very important that you have your resilience toolbox ready to help you move on. How so, you ask? Read on.

NEW ATTITUDES FOR A RESILIENT LIFE

First, you may slowly find your inner circle of friends shifting right along with your newfound life. Negative, stuck people don't want your life to be held up as a reflection of their failings (they are the ones holding it up not you). Now combine this with general attitudes and unexpected behaviors of people you may encounter along the way who live unconsciously and may attempt to use you as a punching bag for their frustrations. You have to be ready for the negative people who live on standby just to rattle your cage.

You will need to put up your personal shield to block out that stuff, which is why recognition and celebration of who you are and how far you've come will be an important reminder to stay the course and avoid the distractions. When you're resilient, it no longer matters if you have an off day. It doesn't matter if some random stranger says an unkind word or acts disrespectfully toward you. A resilient person will have the stamina to rise up above the junk and see it for what is, refocus on the business at hand, and get back to positive thinking — it's about being confident in who you are, understanding how things/people work, and responding from where you are rather than reacting to circumstances or people who "push your buttons."

For example, I know a woman named Sherry. She has a thriving advertising business that has grown 100 percent (yes, even during this economy) and a great personal life with a beautiful family. Some call her a real dynamo. She bulldozes life with the strength and resilience few possess. She starts every day with a huge smile on her face and embraces her life with zest and passion. She gets up, stares at her vision board with a twinkle in her eye, meditates on her vision for her life, and acknowledges the abundance that surrounds her and summons all good things. When she enters a room, it's hard to miss her big smile and enthusiasm. She always lends positive support to her colleagues and believes in "give first and share always," the eWomen Network (a national organization for women entrepreneurs) mantra. People like to be around Sherry, because she is genuine, authentic and caring.

Sherry deals with a lot of clients in her work. She knows how to sell clients and get contracts signed. Now Sherry recently had a totally crazy client encounter. Henry was a referral from a good friend so in that respect he was vetted before they met. Sherry met with Henry and the meeting went extremely well. He asked that she develop a creative brief for his campaign. Sherry readily agreed and produced the brief. When Henry received the brief, he called a meeting. Sherry arrived ready to sign a contract with Henry to develop his entire advertising campaign. During the meeting, things suddenly went south. Henry started ripping on Sherry's brief telling her it was like reading a "really lame boiler." He proceeded to go off about its lack of originality and creativity. Sherry was embarrassed as Henry berated and yelled at her. Completely stunned and taken off guard, Sherry extricated herself out of the meeting — but she felt emotionally "slimed."

Although Sherry knew better, she had a great deal of difficulty getting his criticism out of her head. She rehashed the conversation in her mind; searched for what she said or did that might have set him off; wondered if the brief (that she worked very hard to create) was really "lame;" and questioned herself and her competence and skill. Henry's negativity consumed her for a day — even though she had just received some amazing news on another account. Sherry slept on it and bounced back the very next day — she allowed herself to feel her feelings, and in doing so processed them out of her system in a healthy way. But most people "stuff" their feelings, wallow in them, and never bounce back.

Sherry is the perfect example of how even the most resilient individual can fall off the emotional wagon and get dragged down. Sherry is super resilient though. After realizing that she could not please everyone, she abandoned the self doubt in favor of renewed confidence. She demanded of herself to fill the tracks in her head that Henry's words had set off and focus on thinking about her visions and goals instead. Soon, Henry's words turned into the annoying "fly" that she managed to squash with a swatter.

Please understand that Sherry's rebound isn't that easy to accomplish. I will tell you straight up, you may find it ridiculously difficult not to be distracted by negativity and nasty behavior. You may find yourself questioning whether you're doing the right thing. You may be criticized for your amazing attitude in a subtle way. You may find that some people are just negative — and your positive attitude annoys them; it may even give them cause to attack you. They may feel jealous or resentful of your success, because they know and can feel your energetic shift. They secretly wish you ill ... but none of these reasons will make you feel any better when they attack. At this point, you may buy into all the nonsense. You might feel doubts. All that garbage may feed into some secret anxiety or fears you have about yourself. You may try vigilantly to shake it off, but it feels difficult — almost impossible.

The more resilient you are, the more self aware you become; the more committed you become to being your authentic self, and the more you tune into the universe and understand the Laws of Attraction, the less likely you are to get snared in a mental trap set by other people. You don't have to have a negative view of people — you just have to understand that not everyone has learned your lessons. Not everyone has come to understand the principles of resilience.

They are still chasing their tails. You cannot let people who would secretly enjoy seeing you fail get close enough to cause harm. Someone yells at you for any reason, you walk away. You don't stand there and let the negativity seep in. You stay away from it, and you remind yourself of all of the wonderful, positive strides you have made in your new life. You celebrate all forward motion. You acknowledge the beauty that surrounds you every day. Show gratitude and thank God for all of it — every day.

PERSONAL VIGILANCE FOR ONGOING RESILIENCE

Here's the most important piece of advice: *Stay vigilant when choosing the people you want to be around; and be super vigilant when it comes to accepting what they say — you stand guard at the gate of your mind and keep negative thoughts and ideas out*. Pay very close attention to the underlying messages. Keep negativity and naysayers away from you.

Let me give you an example of subtle behavior to watch for. Annie is a famous writer. She has everything to be proud about — best-selling books and a thriving literary career. Annie sits in a writer's circle with a woman named "Rhonda," who is also a dynamic, driven and talented writer. Rhonda has done some incredible things, and when the discussion turns to her she excitedly tells the group what is going on with her latest project. Just about every time Rhonda discusses her next project, Annie always makes some kind of "cute" cutting or divisive remark. Annie for whatever reason (one that absolutely makes no sense given her impressive accomplishments) feels threatened by Rhonda. At first, Rhonda didn't notice. She, like the rest of the group, would laugh along with the "cute" but clearly cutting jokes. It soon became a pattern. Rhonda became more aware and awake to the comments. She realized she needed to get out of the group, as this kind of negativity didn't serve her. She didn't need to make a stink about it, but just left the group. Now why not confront Annie versus leave? People like Annie who possess such deep insecurities and lack self-awareness about these insecurities cannot be reasoned with or "fixed."

If you encounter similar situations you have to realize you would be fighting someone's years of built up issues that are not your challenge to fix. You are better off to focus on yourself, your vision, and move forward. Other groups exist where healthier attitudes prevail. Switch groups and take the high road. You will always feel better than engaging in a war of words with someone doomed to their own cage full of garbage they just don't know how to take out.

IT GETS EASIER

It has taken many years for me to grow and become resilient. I know this book may make it sound like all you have to do is read the words and "zap" you're resilient and happy. I understand it takes more than a book to push you out of years of patterns that brought you to the bookstore to pick up my book. I get it; but it is truly through taking small steps forward, acknowledging every little accomplishment, and continuing your progress that you will become a naturally resilient person — sometimes without consciously thinking about it. It has taken me years of working on myself to come to where I am now; and I continue on my journey, striving to be better and better.

I am now resilient every day, but this kind of resilience requires a lot of heavy lifting on my part. I am constantly reminding myself and using the tools I am sharing with you — this isn't a fix-it-and-go type of work, this is a lifestyle — a way of being. I take time to exercise, meditate, and go for walks to marvel at the abundance and wisdom God wants me to have. I understand that I attract the positive things in my life. I know that if I focus on what I don't want I will receive what I focus on. I apply the Laws of Attraction. And most importantly, I am grateful for all of it — good or not so good. It doesn't matter anymore. I know it is my journey. I know that within the challenges are the lessons. It now excites me when something happens, and I realize there is a message for me. You need to understand that beneath all the hurts and pains lay positive, uplifting and meaningful lessons meant to teach us and increase our wisdom, as well as empower us to move on with great confidence.

When we realize that our life's lessons offer us tools for self-empowerment, we cannot be held back or down. We grow and move forward. We celebrate everything and every moment. We thank God even when it doesn't seem obvious that gratitude should be a part of the equation. For example, Michelle's house caught on fire last summer. The fire scorched some heavy equipment and torched the fence. A random passer-by stopped and told Michelle and her husband Russell about the fire. The blaze got put out before it did more harm. Want to know what Michelle thought? "Thank God it didn't get to the main house. Thank God a stranger told us. Thank God my family was unharmed. Thank you God for protecting us." Now this is pure resilience.

Michelle could have reacted just the opposite (notice the word 'reacted') and focused on the cost of the property damage, etc. She could have asked, "Why us?" But, since she practiced 'responding' rather than 'reacting,' Michelle turned inward and acted (responded) from a place of solid resilience. It is what it is, now what do I need to do to move on? This is a great statement/question to keep you focused on the reality of things rather than flying off the handle and causing more harm with a hot temper. Resilient people don't go there!

You too, like Michelle, need to understand that gratitude and thankfulness are possibilities within all things that happen — positive or negative. When you come to this understanding, you will have achieved 100-percent joy and happiness; you are now 100-percent responsible for your life and your results. You can join the ranks of resilient people and begin to enjoy success and abundance at a totally new level. Resilient people are rarely unhappy! Wow! Doesn't that sound just amazing? Don't you want that kind of happiness?

Of course you do. And you can have it, I promise!

Chapter Seven

Maintenance Plan: Reinforcing the New Successful You

"Optimist: Someone who figures
that taking a step backward after taking a step forward
is not a disaster, it's a cha-cha."
— ROBERT BRAULT

Now you've gone and done it — you've prevailed and you're on top of the world. You've realized your vision; you're living the great dream; you've got all those ducks lined up in perfect order; and then every once in a while you become a little nervous. What if *this* is all there is now? What if I have found utopia — and this is it? Now what happens?

Acrobats and Comets are floating by so fast
Children's faces S.M.I.L.E. like suns at last
Lilac butterflies are cruising without fear
All inviting you to stay and rest here
You can halt your car for an afternoon in Utopia.

Those lyrics come straight from alternative band Alphaville. I wish you could hear the actual song in your head — it's beautiful. And the point is that if you've parked your car so close to utopia you're anxious about the close of the day, and maybe you've come this far and you could fall, and then what? Because now you've experienced utopia. You know the difference. Once you know the difference, the alternative is in some way even less attractive to consider than ever before; but at the same time, this repugnance can be a very useful tool to keep you looking forward not backward.

Every bump, every nasty crisis, and every pitfall you ran into that brought you to the here and now — the utopia you've sought — was put there for a reason. While that reason may have not felt wonderful at the time, you must be grateful for it. If you did not fall and learn to brush off the "stuff" that kept you stuck in the status quo, you would have never gotten on the road to utopia. And once in utopia, you have basked in the joy and newfound happiness. So, most importantly, regret none of it. Feel no resentment toward anyone or anything that hurt you or made you angry and sad. You would not be who you are today without those people or events. You would not be doing what you're doing without those experiences. So thank those people or situations — at least in your mind — and then send them on their way back into their world.

As for you, now is the time to embrace what comes your way. Your maintenance plan is summed up in: "what?" What can you do to stay in your own private utopia? The answer is one word: *acceptance.*

Once you've come to a new place in your life and embraced a whole new self-awareness and self-empowerment, it's time to still the waters. It's time to travel your road with calm acceptance. You do not fight anything or anyone. You recognize that new challenges in your new life are all there to help you. When you realize that all of these things become the day's lessons, you can look at it all so differently. It's like twisting the lens on a Kaleidoscope where the refraction of the light changes the scene to reveal a new color or shape. It's beautiful.

When you learn that your vision may take on a slightly different refraction of the light, but it's still your vision, then you can embrace and warm up to the idea that the evolution of your life is beautiful. It's so easy to embrace, love and cherish beautiful things — and this new life will forever be a work in progress with new angles, opportunities and directions all of the time; but if you understand not to cast a negative perspective on it — to instead embrace the changes — you will have found your new "status," and it has nothing to do with "quo."

It is the status of change. It is the status of brilliance. You will also find that your version of utopia just shifts a little and maybe, just maybe, opens to yet something bigger, brighter and beyond expectations. You may actually find that something you didn't include in the original vision becomes possible, probable and even inevitable. You may pinch yourself when your dream blows up into something wild and wonderful; but let me tell you something: The opening in the road of your life will keep being so wildly wonderful and amazing, because you put to rest all the negative stuff that held you back. You learn to think about everything through that slightly twisted, yet still gorgeous lens of positivity. Because the purpose of this book isn't just to teach you about resilience — it's to empower you to become resilient and positive — and transform this into your own "coming-of-you" story.

Those of you who are new to these concepts may think that this sounds great and all; but you can't feel the same exhilaration or, more importantly, "understand" this feeling until you've been there. The feeling of finding yourself is incredible. And that is what this book is truly about — finding out who you are underneath the "stuff" and allowing a liberation of self. Bringing out the person who is perfect in God's eyes and designed to be utterly and perfectly flawed. Yes, you heard it. We are designed to be beautifully imperfect in this imperfect world — and to bask in the perfection of imperfection. You can sit right now and let your own exhilaration wash over you like warm water, smile, close your eyes and ... just feel it. You may even feel a soft sob well up in your throat and warm tears fall effortlessly down your cheeks. That's OK. You've discovered something in that moment. You've discovered you. You've accepted you ... beautiful, "perfect" YOU!

Acceptance — when you accept, you invite in. You allow and you do something even more important ... you embrace. You're OK just the way you are ... your life *is* utopia. Right now it might not be quite to that visionary point, but by all means, here in the now, it's a grand thing. And now bow your head or look up and send gratitude. Thank God for all of it. Gratitude and blessings line the walls of your life; tears of joy stream through the middle; and love of who you are now and who you will be tomorrow … love for all people and things that brought you here … all of these gifts now hold you tight. You cannot fall from grace or lose anything when you feel this complete and utter warmth of the truth. When you love you; when you accept you … and most of all when you respond with a thank you and a gesture of unconditional kindness … well, then you have learned what you set out to learn when you picked up this book. *"Love is the thing you know,"* says Louis to Carrie in the original *Sex in the City* movie — and it is!

Conclusion

After the Recession ...
Success Beyond Imagination

Have you ever heard the expression, what goes up must come down? Well, what goes down must also come up — and soon this recession will recede (pun intended). The absolutely fantastic news is that while the coming of the end is inevitable, your life after the recession is not quite as obvious as it once used to be. You are not the same person you were when the fall from financial grace began. You have followed your transformational journey to a new life and a new you; you are so far ahead of those who sat in their status-quo world, waiting, wondering and worrying when it would end. Maybe those folks made do and got by

OK, but one thing they did not do was reinvent and transform — become a magical, amazing and, most importantly, flexible versions of who they once were.

This recession without a doubt has changed millions of lives. Generation V as mentioned earlier didn't need the recession to tell them this was not how they were intended to live. Other people who got shoved into an awakening that was transformative feel totally blessed and might even acknowledge they're glad this happened to them. And these two groups today are poised to reap the emotional, physical and financial benefits sure to come their way. The end of the recession will leave them with new careers built and set to flourish and move up the corporate ladder; new businesses already successful and geared to leap to the next level; new family lives full of peace, connection and love; and an entirely remodeled way of life where passion and purpose lead the way toward fulfillment and happiness. These people are set to reap the benefits of overflowing blessings and, essentially, cherries on top of cherries on their overloaded sundaes. Yet all of this overflow was not necessarily the point, it is merely a bonus — the icing on the moist, already-delicious cake.

How this emerging demographic of "recession survivors" will feel about what is simply more abundance will vary; but the lessons will forever have changed their lives. It imbues their lives with a deeper meaning and understanding of what it is to be successful in this world. It will highlight for them right choices, ability to persevere regardless of the odds, and the idea that success and personal fulfillment do not come from an external set of circumstances. True, wholesome success is a state of mind. Outside environment, conditions and circumstances are a mere reflection of such state of mind — a way of *being.*

If you are one of these people and the recession has ended by the time you read this book then you're already aware of the shift. All of the work you put in is now paying off in spades — and this is not just a wishful prediction, it is a sure outcome. And maybe by the time the financial success has rushed in like a tsunami, you will be in a position to look at it so much differently than you might have done just five years ago. You will value not the financial change, but the personal change brought on by the change in the economy.

I know so many people who are now on completely different and often unexpected tracks than just five or even 10 years ago. Two brand new authors who used to work in the real estate industry would not have had the courage, time or energy to pursue this dream had they not 'lost their jobs.' Yet they embraced their lives and corrected their courses to follow their passions. They are now full-fledged writers out on tour. As their book slowly creeps toward a best seller and the economy changes, do not expect them to jump back into the real estate field. They found out who they were during this economic crisis. They unearthed some important dreams buried beneath their busy lives. Had the recession not stopped them in their tracks, they may have continued on that road; but now they are on this new journey, and they will not give it up — whether the economy rebounds or not! Their story is like so many other stories out there. They found their place in the world. A place that shined a light on the people they always wanted to be — now the people they are. Their priorities shifted. Their desires shifted. Their goals shifted. Their lives shifted. And with the recession over, everything will just expand and expand.

In the end, the lessons learned offer extraordinary insight for so many people. The a-ha moments will not evaporate with full bank accounts but add that extra layer of knowledge to take their lives to the next level. Michelle, who launched a publishing company in the middle of the recession and realized so many dreams, notes that she expects the end of the recession will bring on such an overflow of business that her company will only flourish more. Yet she, like so many others, will manage this overflow differently than before. She has learned to be open and prepared to move forward and embrace opportunities she never thought possible. So many lessons learned now prepare her to deal with the next phase of the business — and at the same time, she looks forward to the day when she can breathe a little easier and watch her company grow with a little less "fertilizer."

If you are one of these people, prepare to reap your well-deserved rewards. Prepare for the journey to become a little easier but *never less meaningful* — be happy that you had this experience. And congratulations! You are recession-proof! Going forward, you will never again worry or concern yourself with external circumstances. You've arrived at your new normal — and it feels great.

So this book is dedicated to all those who learned to change; those who did change; and those who will never be the same again. God bless the recession!

"Set a goal to become a millionaire
for what it will make of you to achieve it."
— JIM ROHN

About the Author

Since early 2006, Selwa has immersed herself in training and practicing as a Life Coach. She is a licensed, independent Business and Life Coach, certified through several coaching experts and programs including: Kitty Cole, Bob Proctor (LifeSuccess Consultants), Holli Walker (180 Life & Style Coaching), and Brian Tracy (Business Growth Strategies). Through Selwa's coaching, her clients are able to focus on their dreams and goals, bring harmony back to their life's endeavors, and move through challenges that were overwhelming without her support and expertise. Selwa continues to develop her coaching through ongoing courses and certifications and stays connected to her community as a graduate of Leadership Napa Valley (2008-2009; Class XXII) and as a member of local Chambers of Commerce and eWomenNetwork.